Dislocation (dislokǎı·ʃən). [a. OF. *dislocation* (14th c. in Littré), or ad. med.L. *dislocātiŏn-em*, n. of action f. *dislocāre* to DISLOCATE.] The action of dislocating, or condition of being dislocated.

1. Displacement; removal from its proper (or former) place or location.

2. *fig.* Displacement of parts or elements; dis- arrangement (of something immaterial); a con- fused or disordered state.

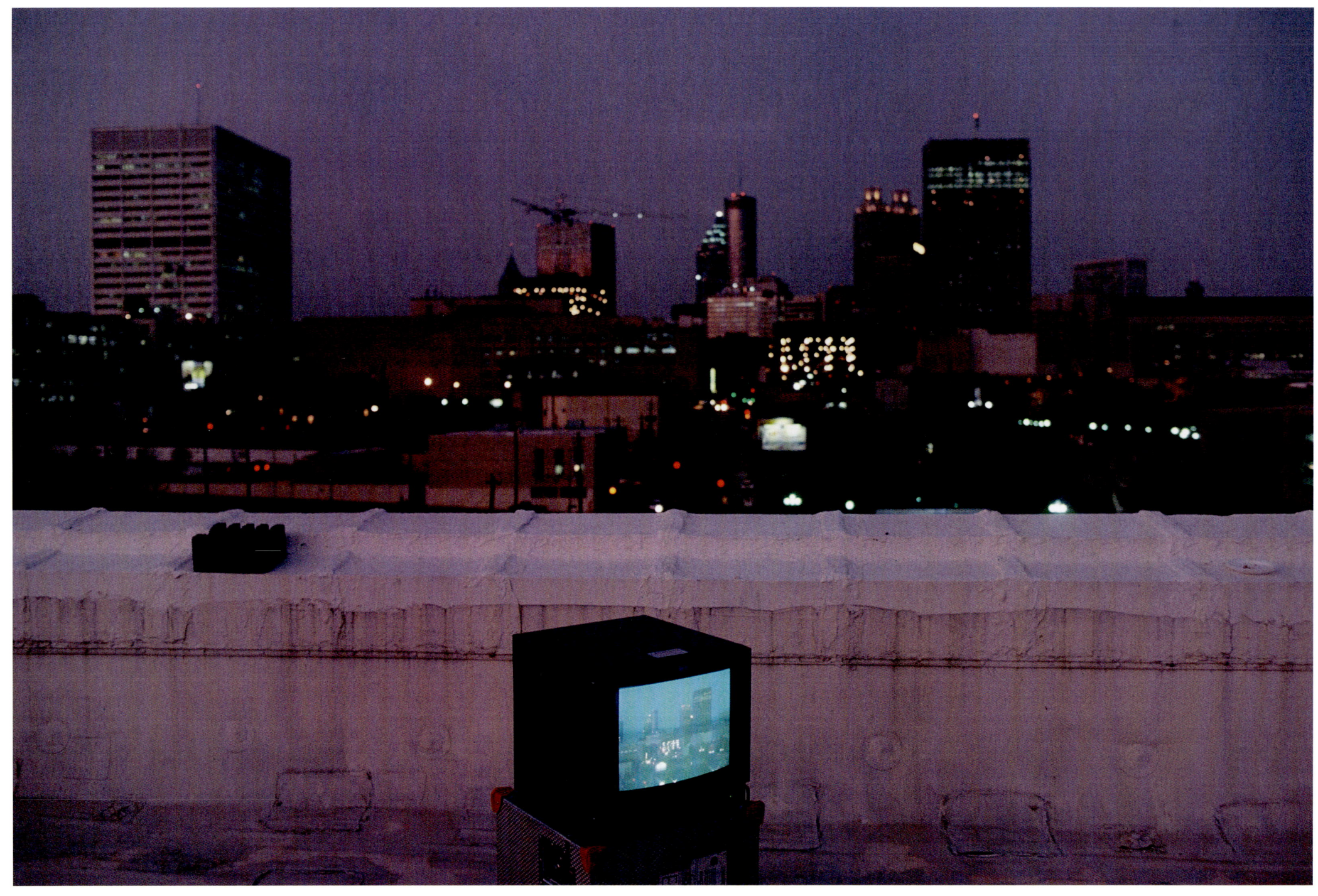

Atlanta, 1996

Dislocations

ALEX WEBB

aperture

"The flow is constant," Alfonse said.

"Words, pictures, numbers, facts, graphics, statistics, specks, waves, particles, motes.

Only a catastrophe gets our attention."

DON DELILLO, *White Noise*

Buffalo, New York, 2017

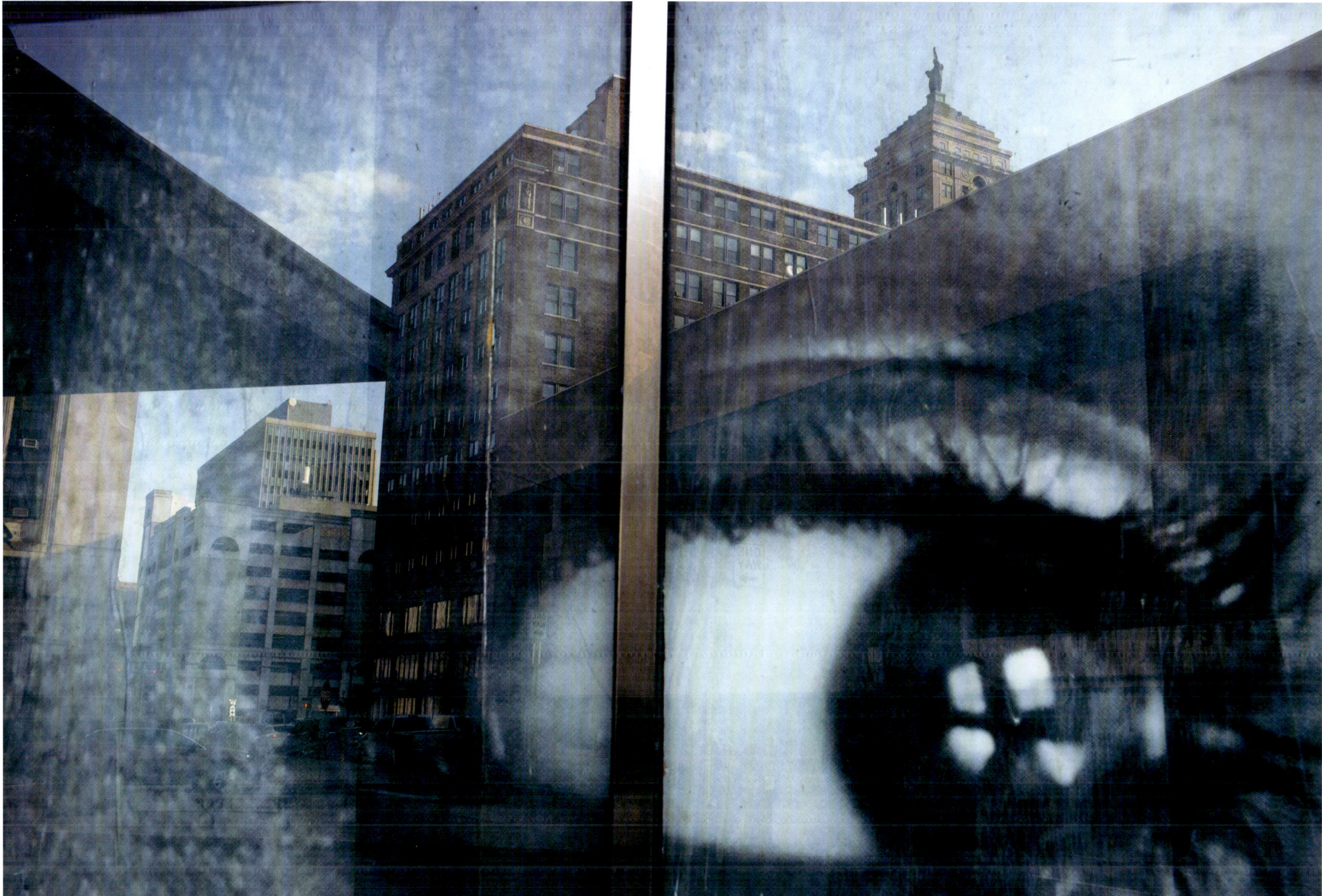

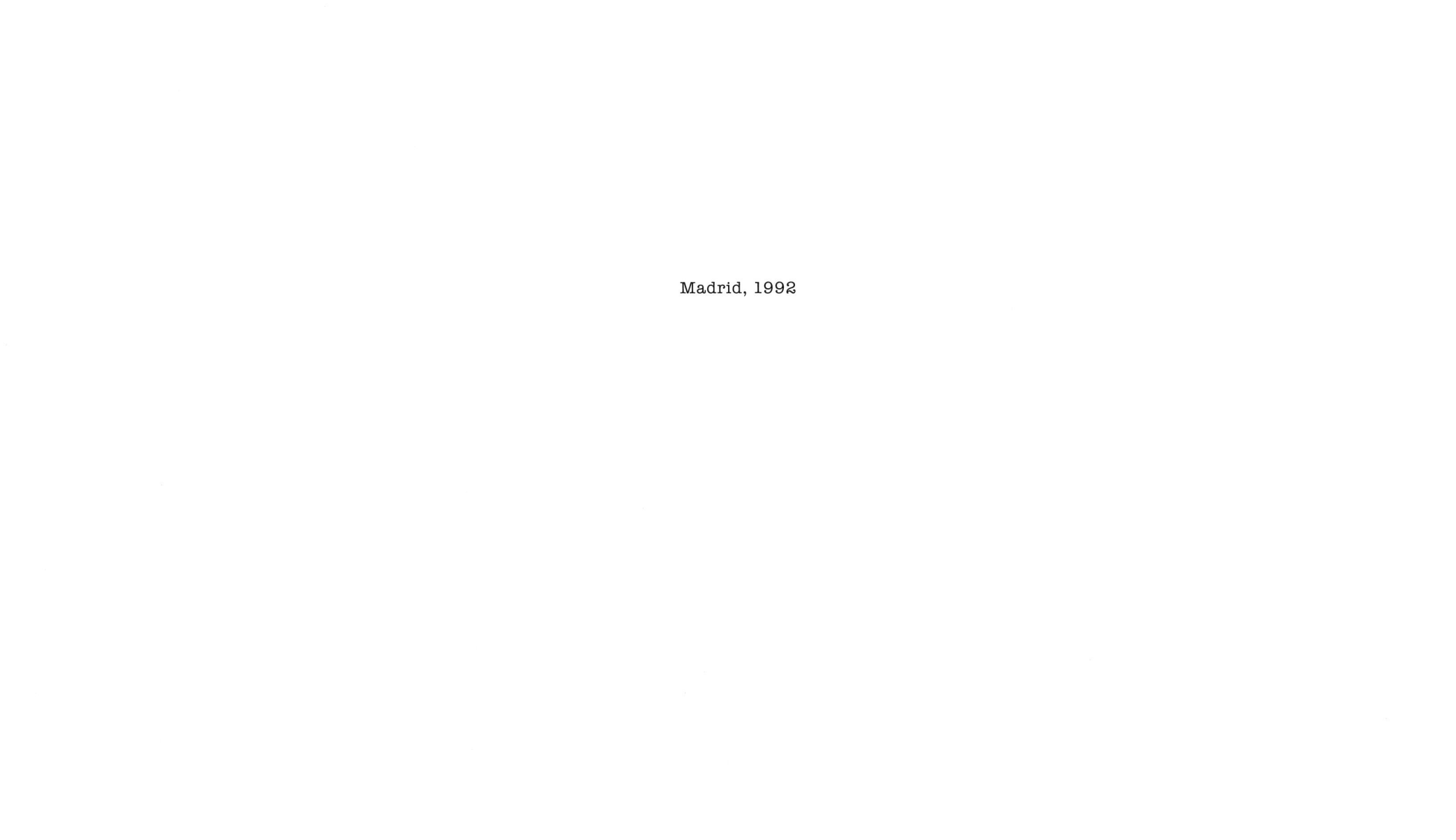

Madrid, 1992

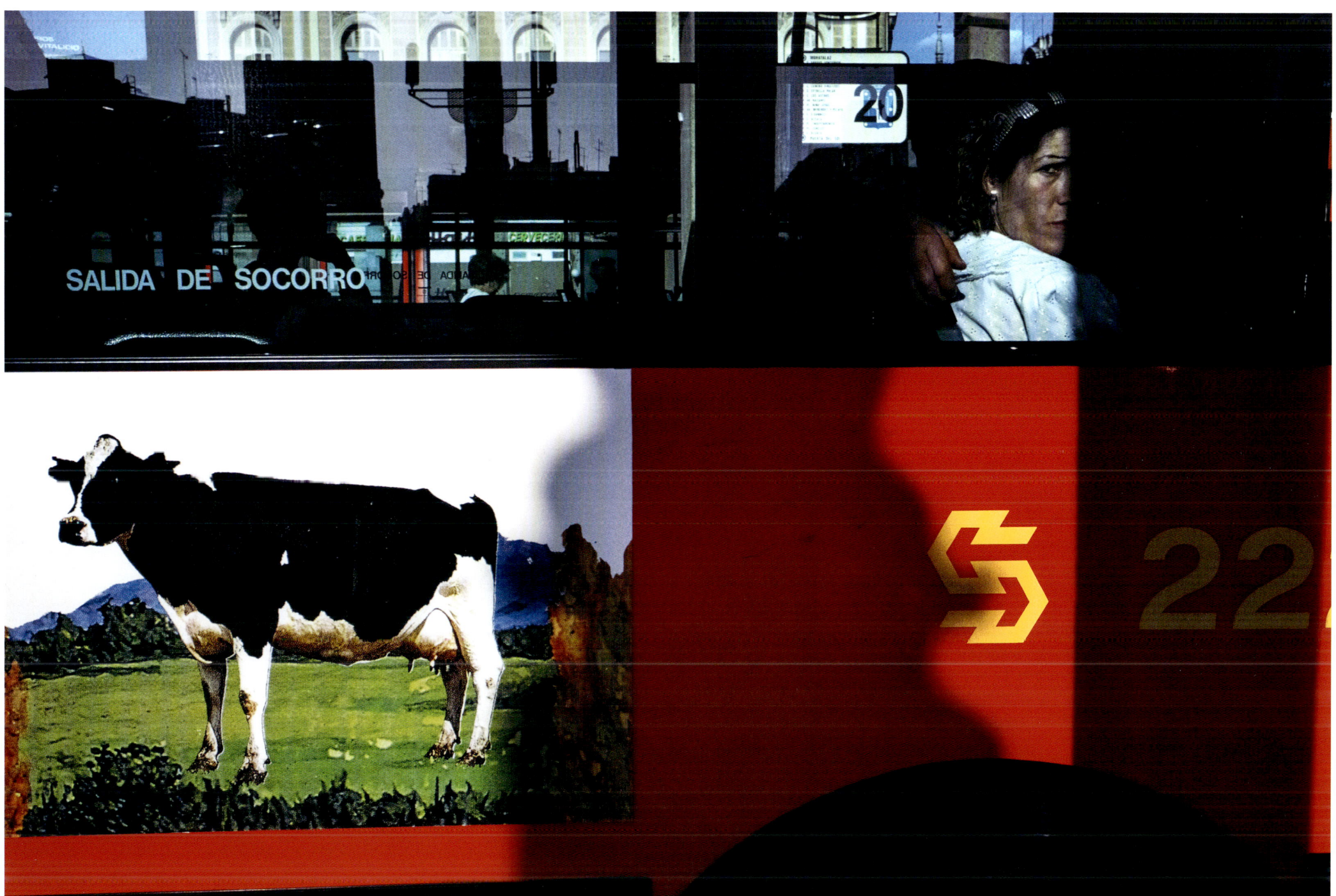

Moscow, 2019

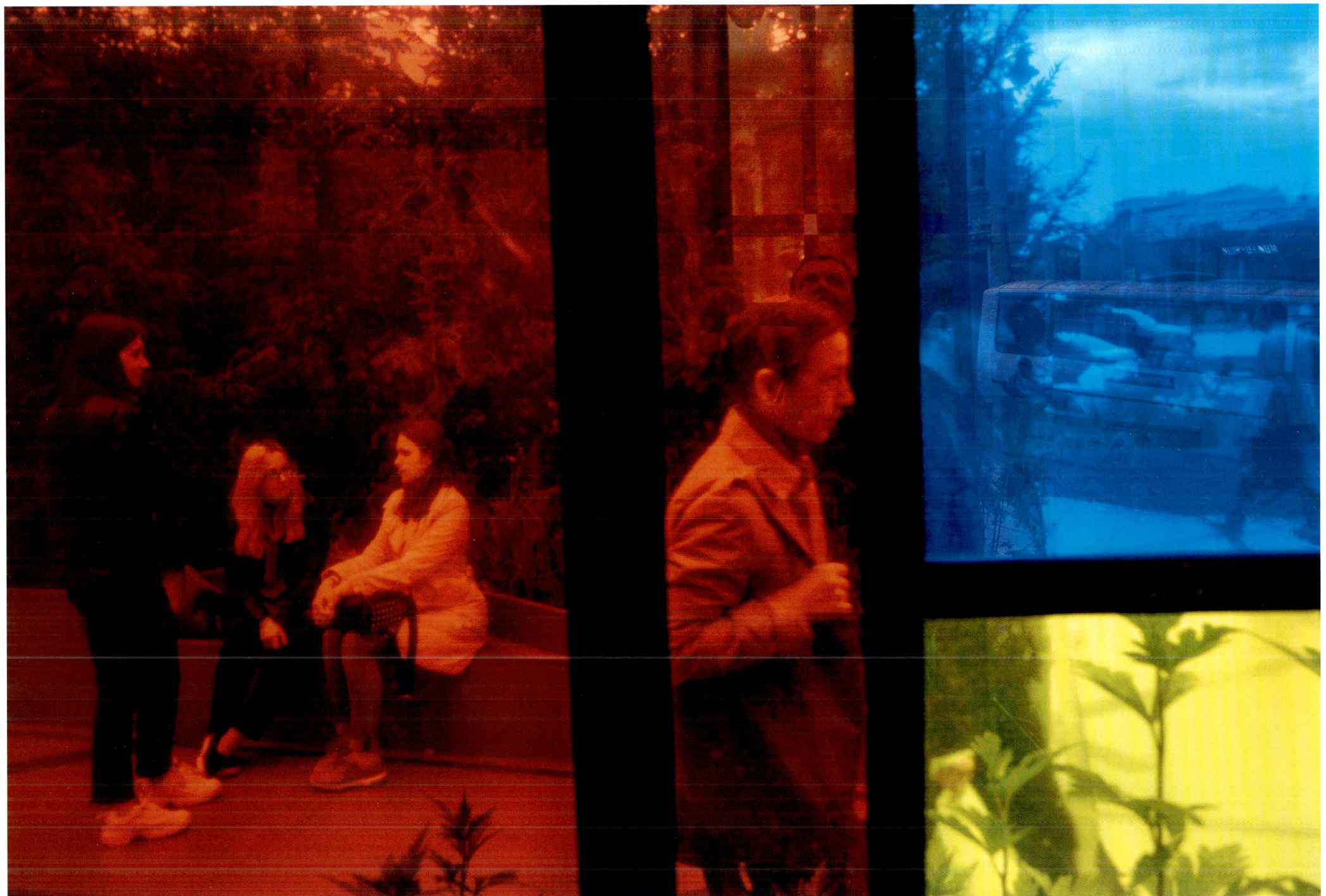

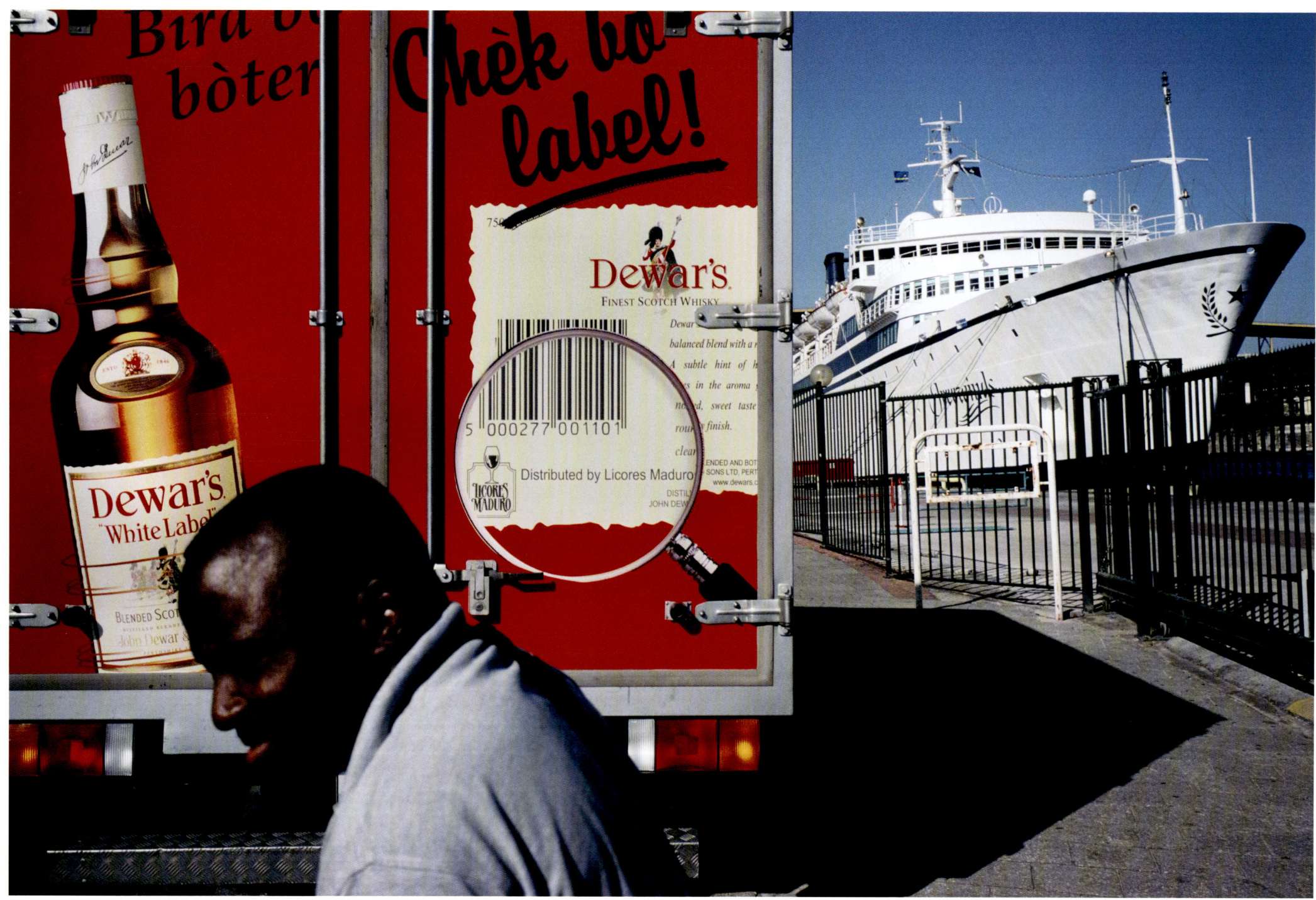

Willemstad, Curaçao, 2010

Chongqing, China, 2017

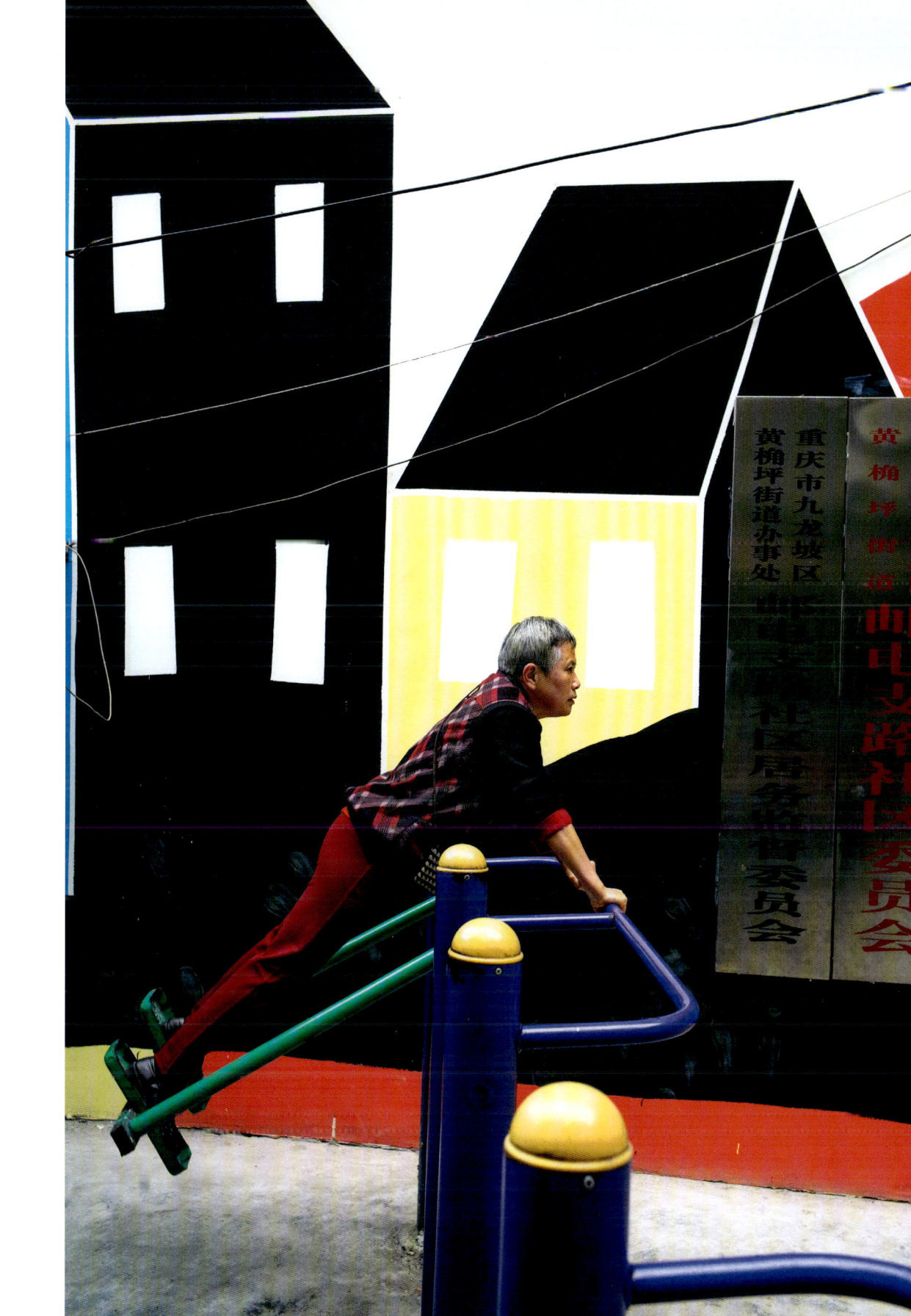

Genoa, Italy, 2019

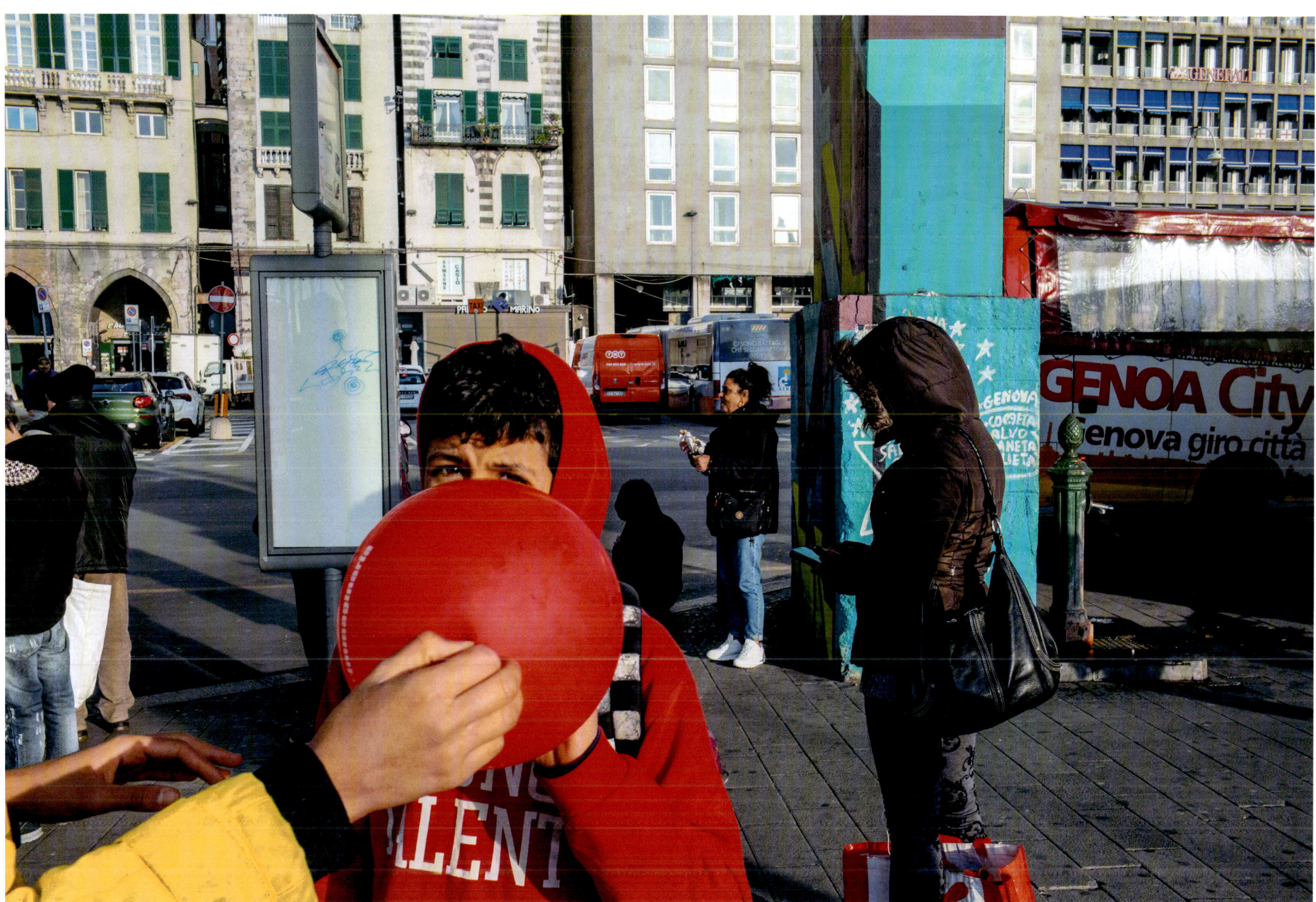

Munich, 1991

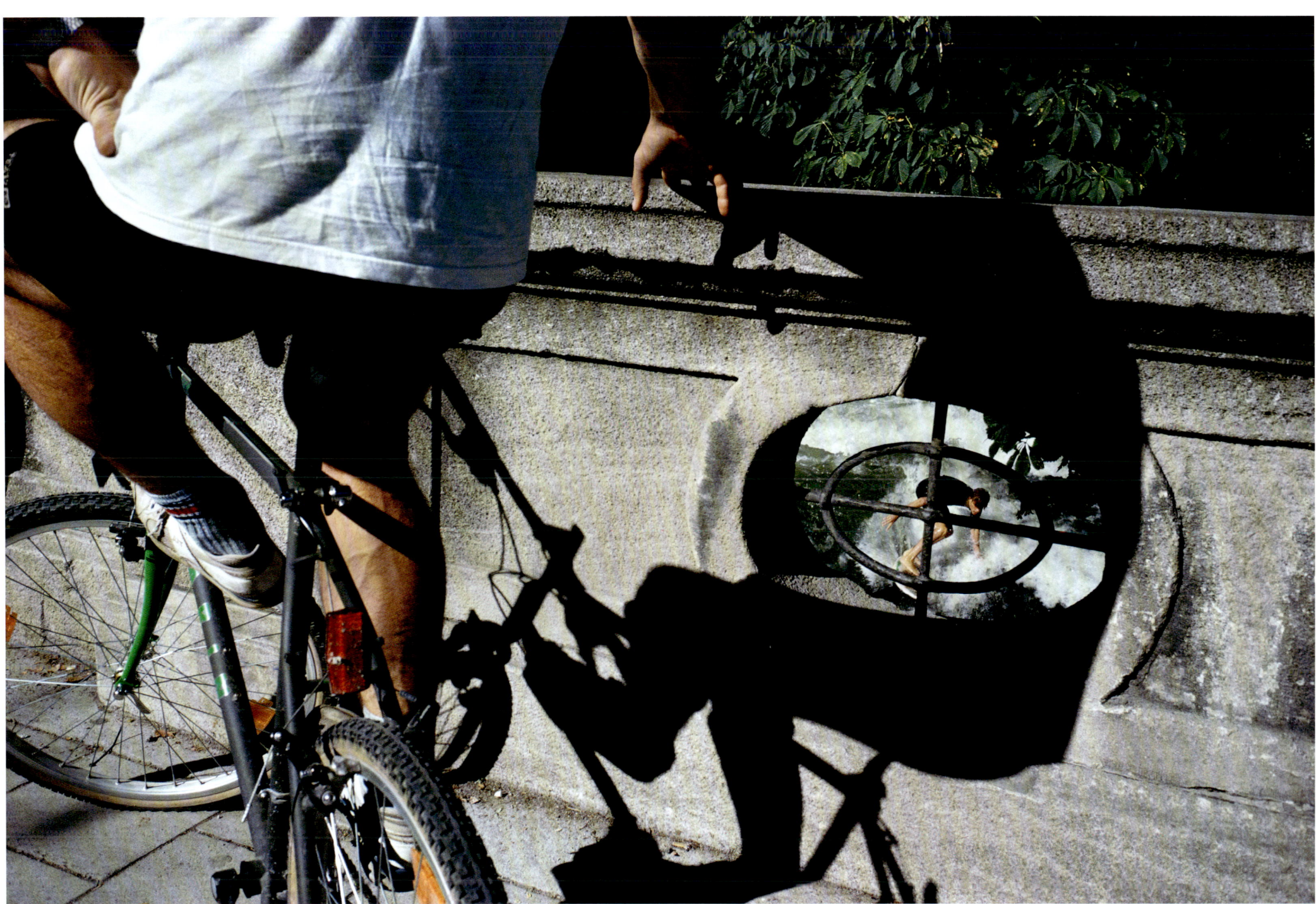

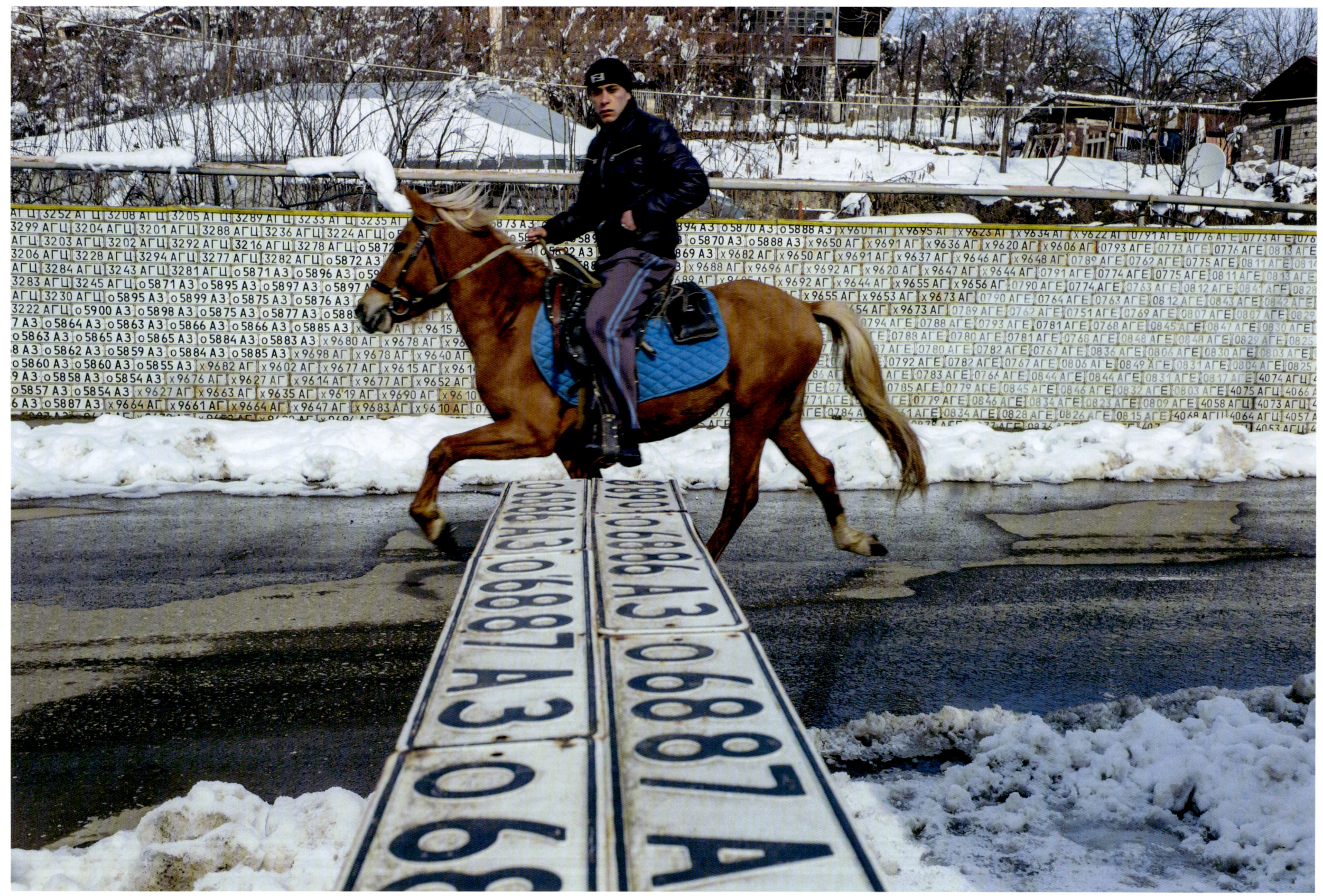

Vank, Nagorno-Karabakh, 2010

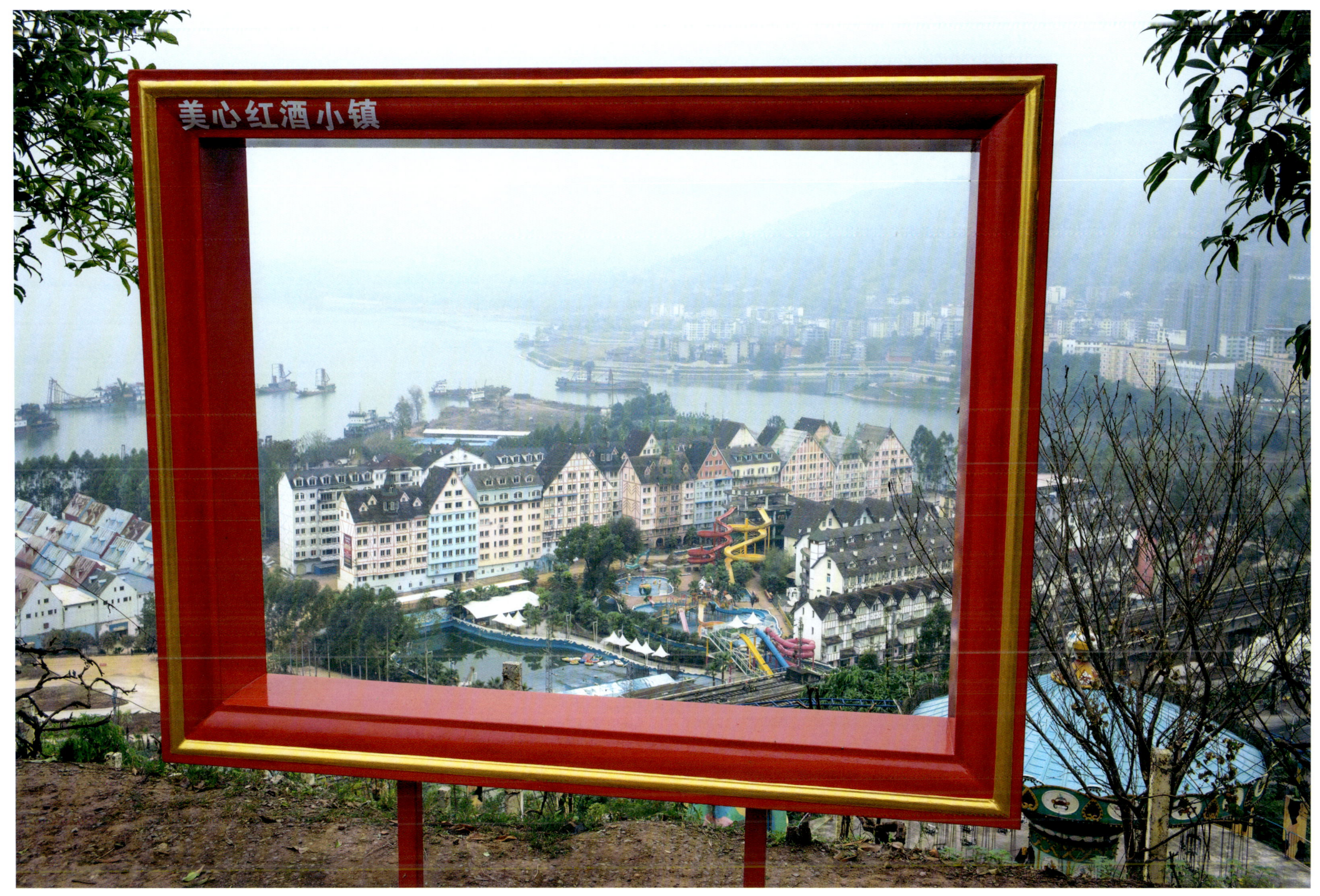

Chongqing, China, 2017

Dallas, 1981

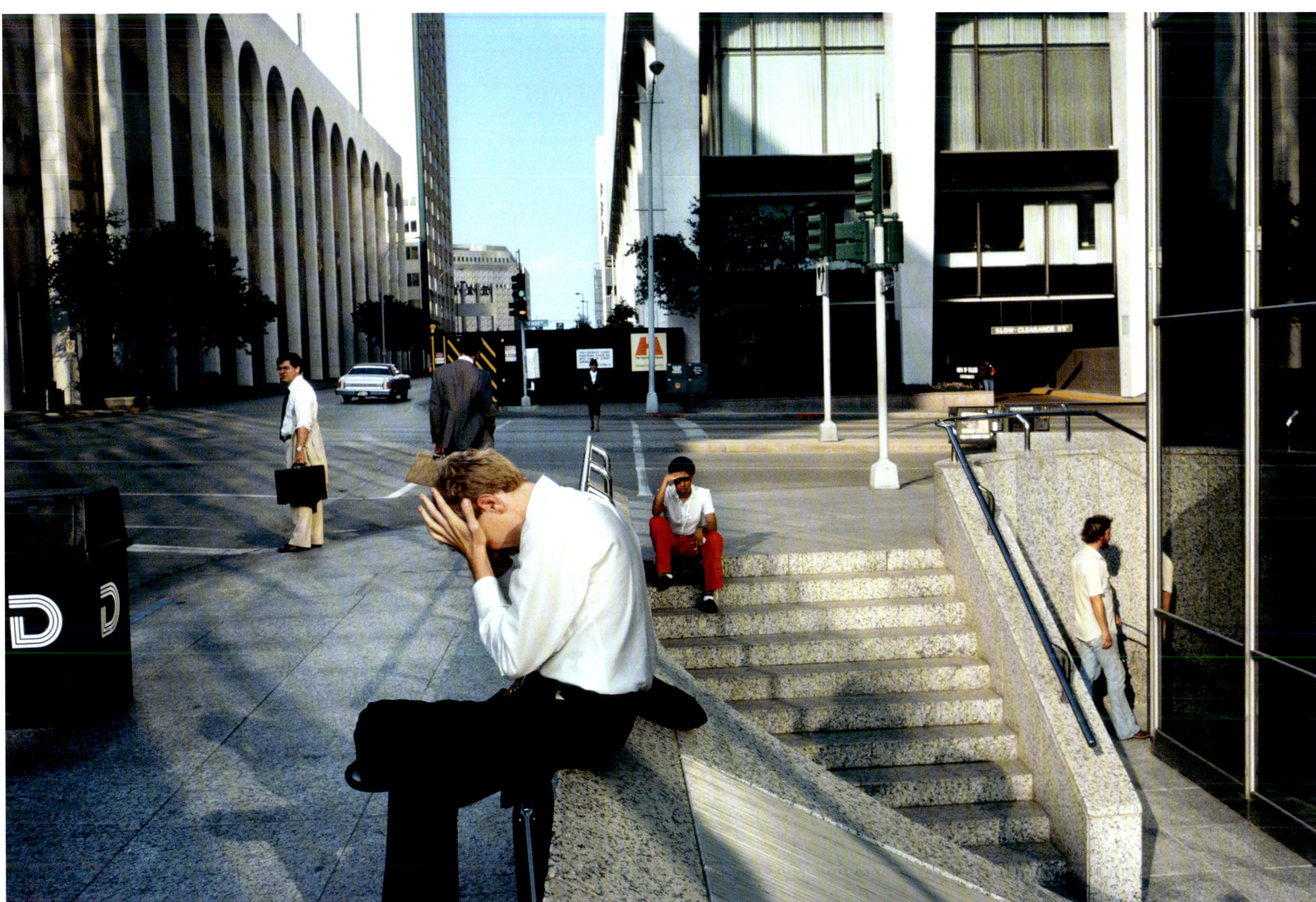

Madrid, 1992

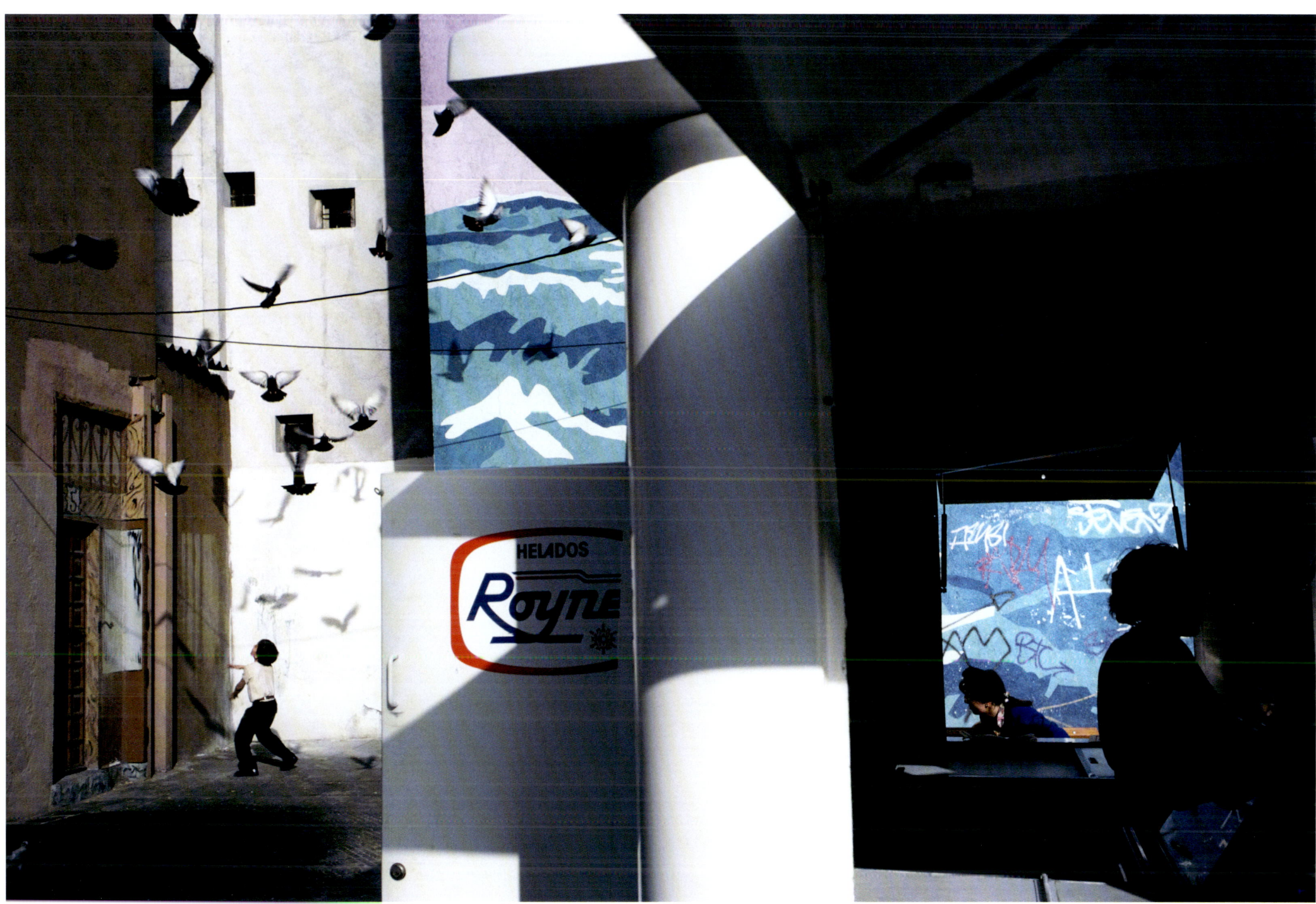

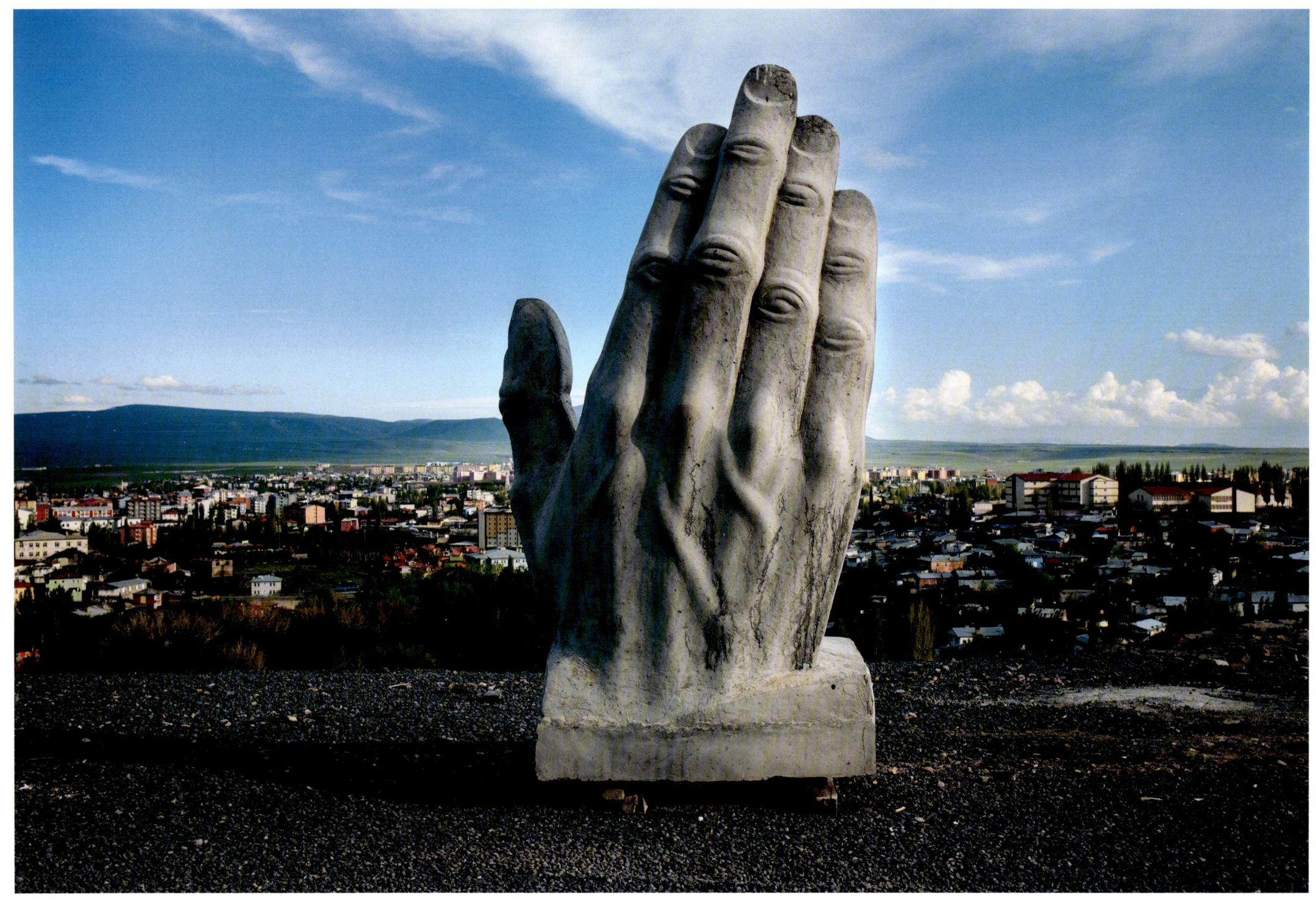

Kars, Turkey, 2009

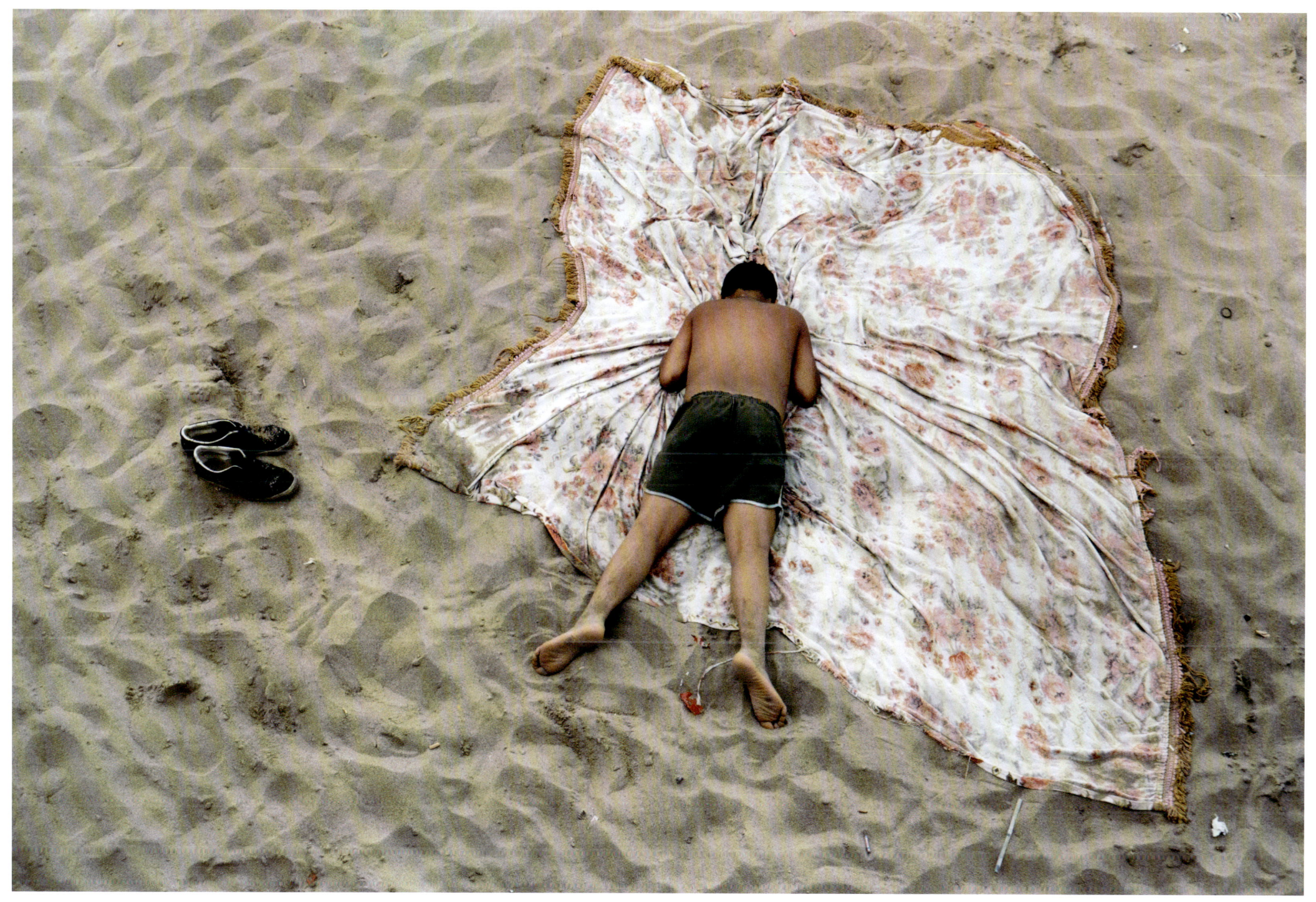

Coney Island, New York, 1983

Fort McMurray, Canada, 2005

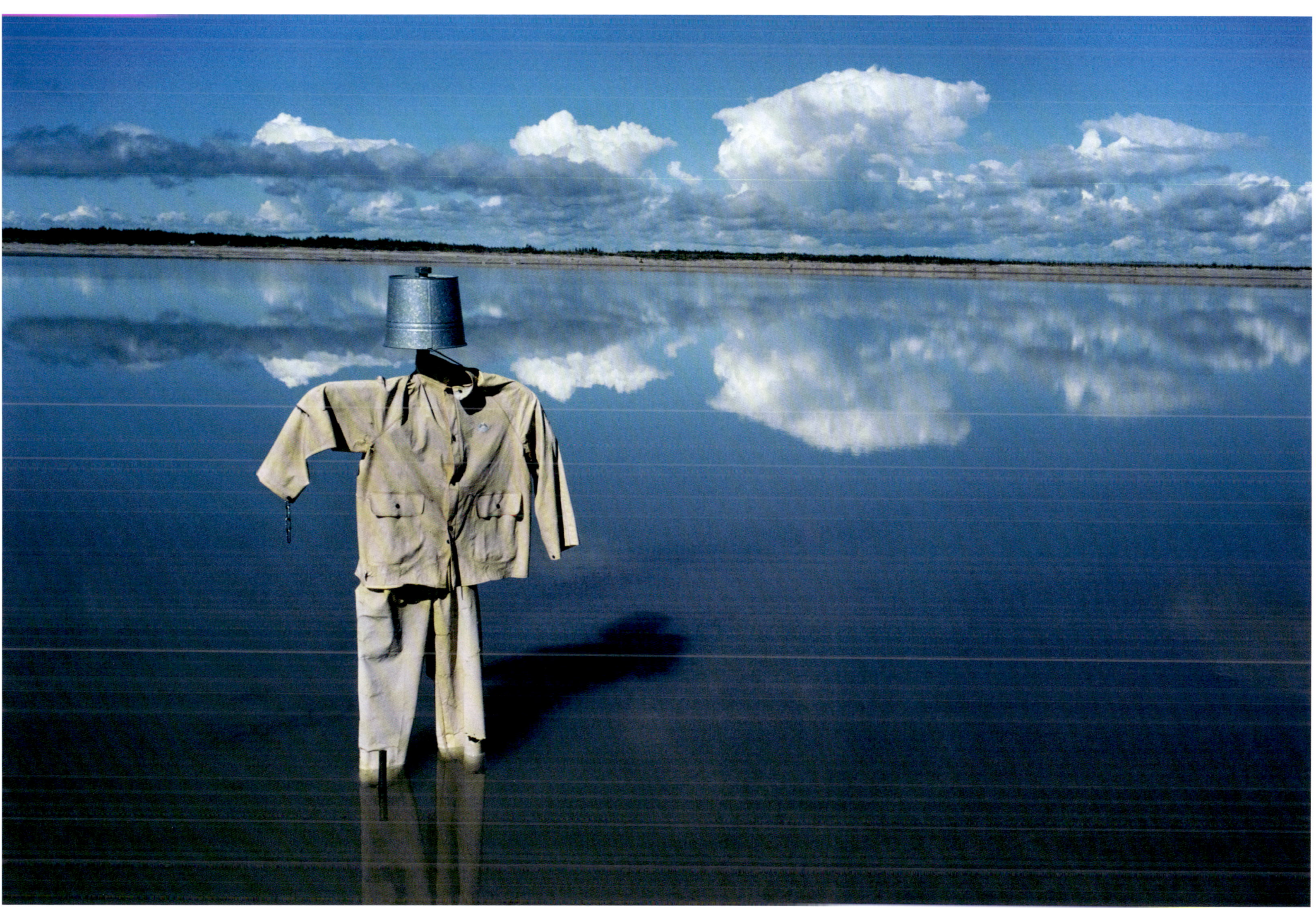

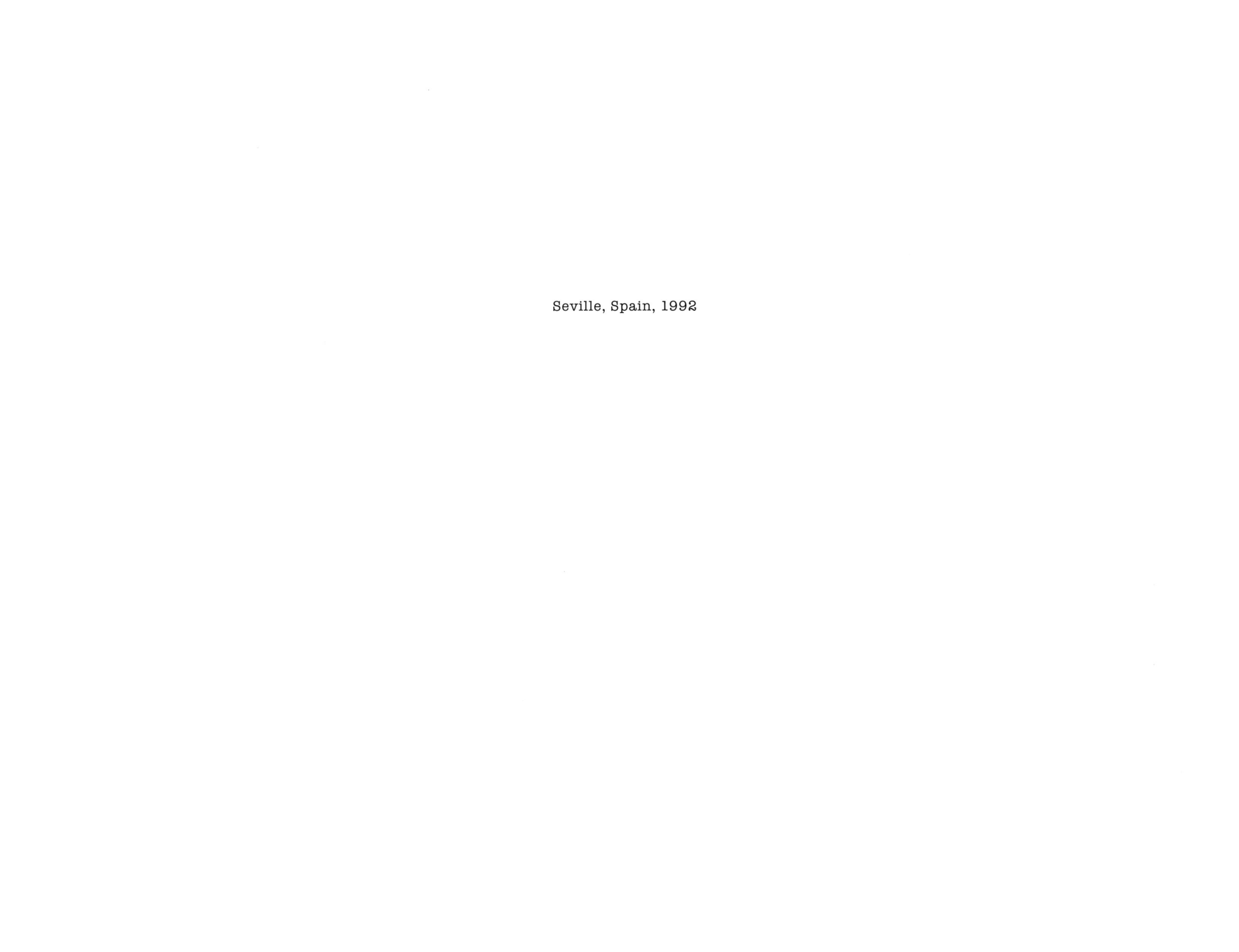

Seville, Spain, 1992

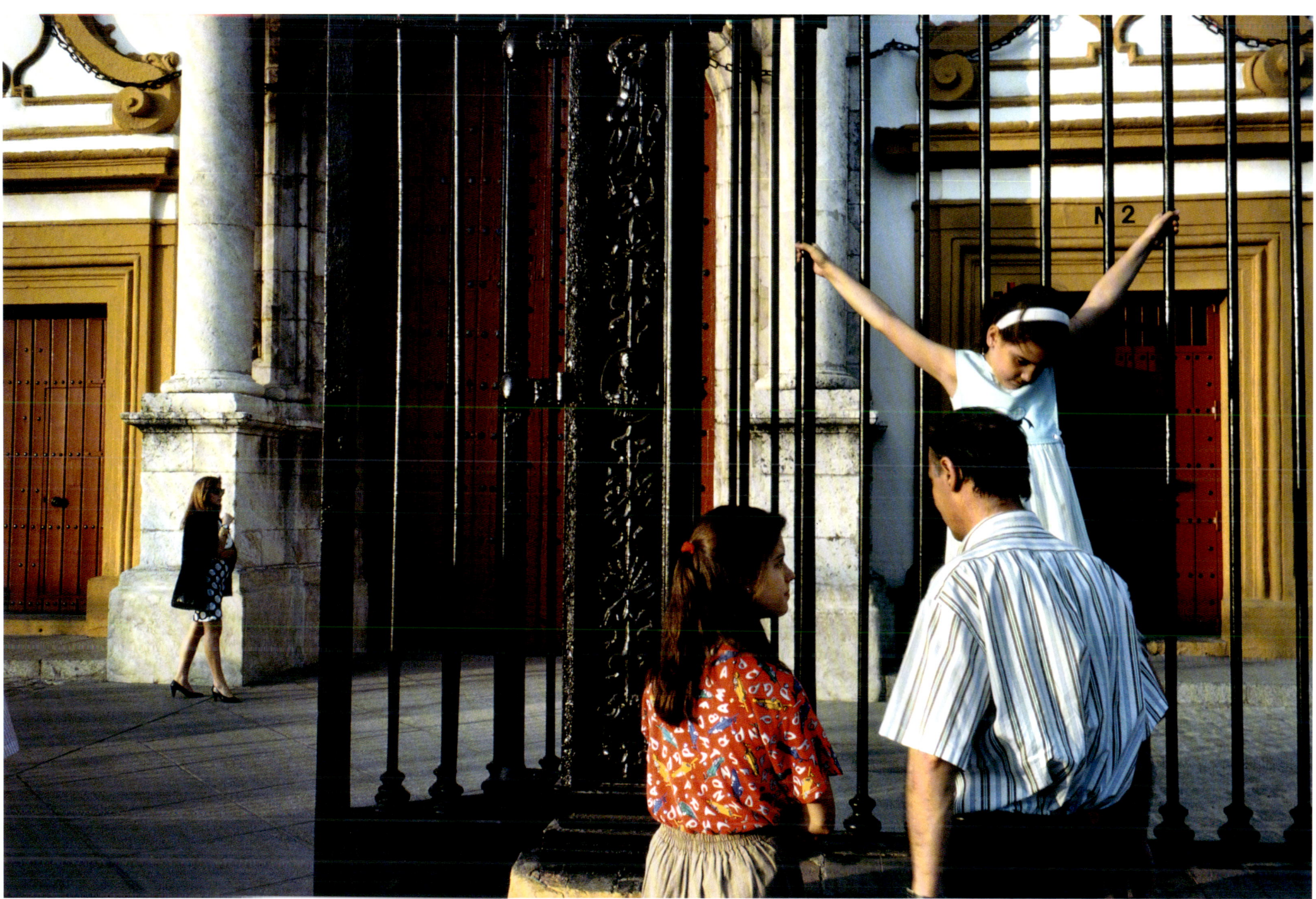

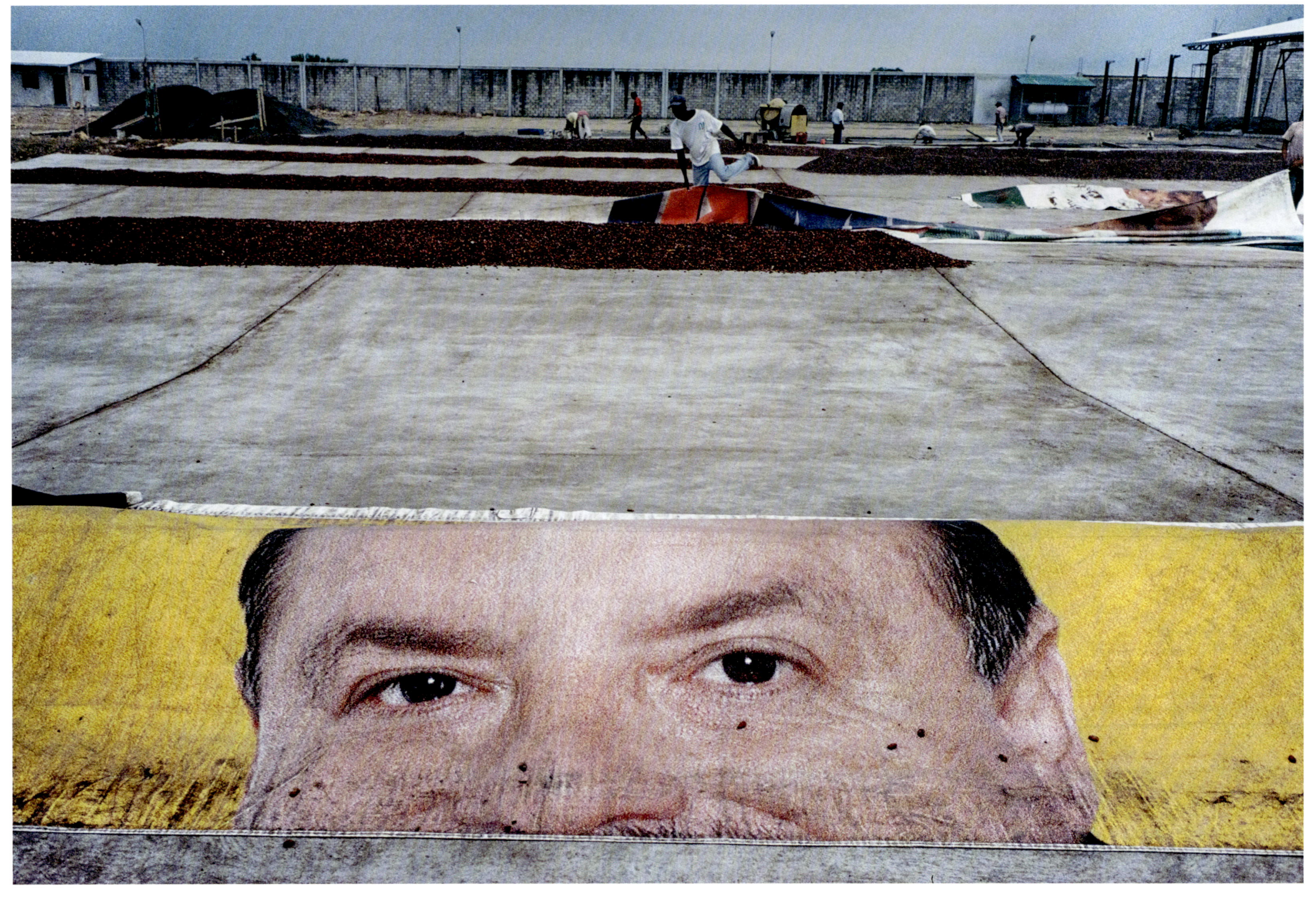

Near Durán, Ecuador, 2002

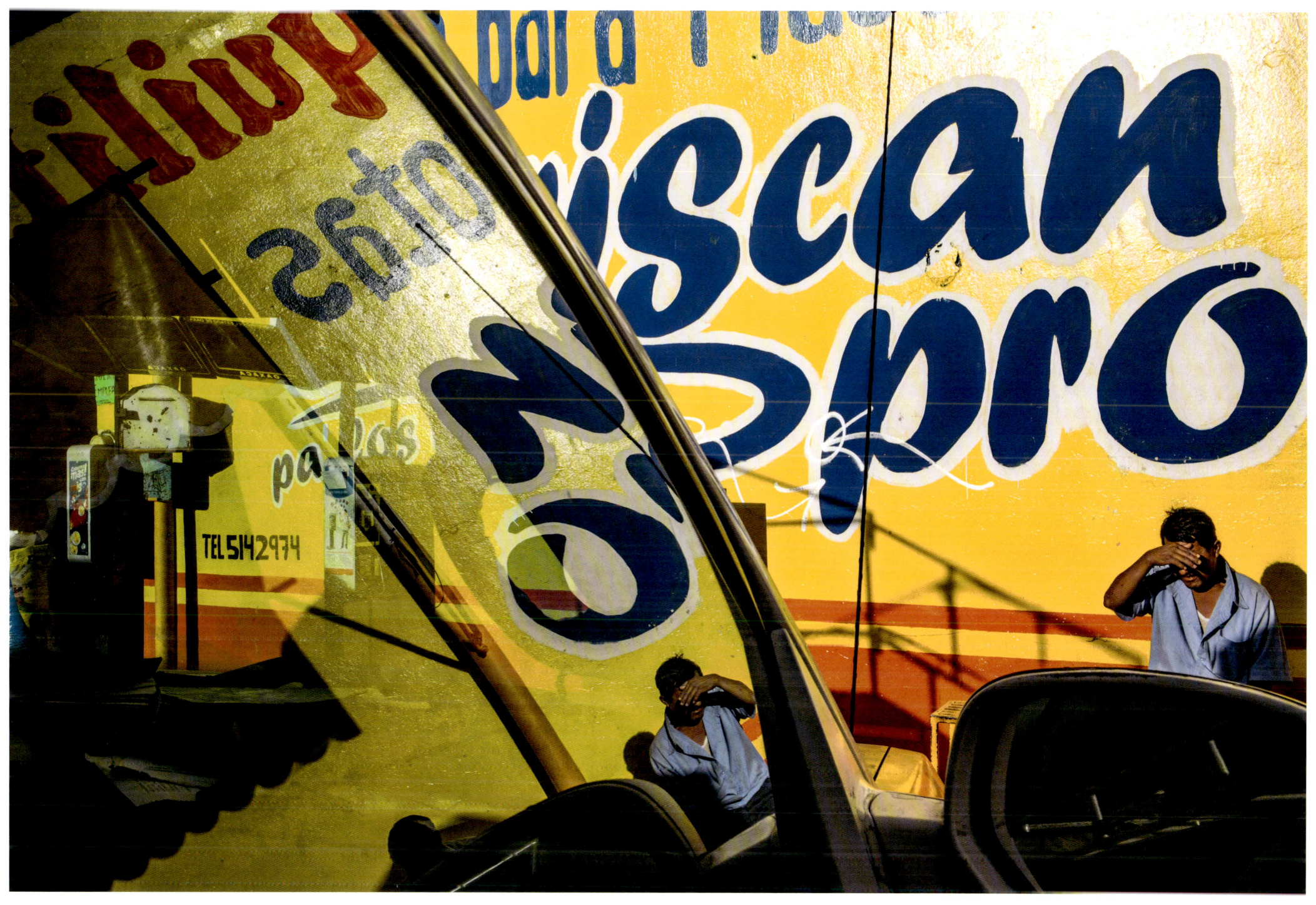

Oaxaca, Mexico, 2018

Tuxtla Gutiérrez, Mexico, 2017

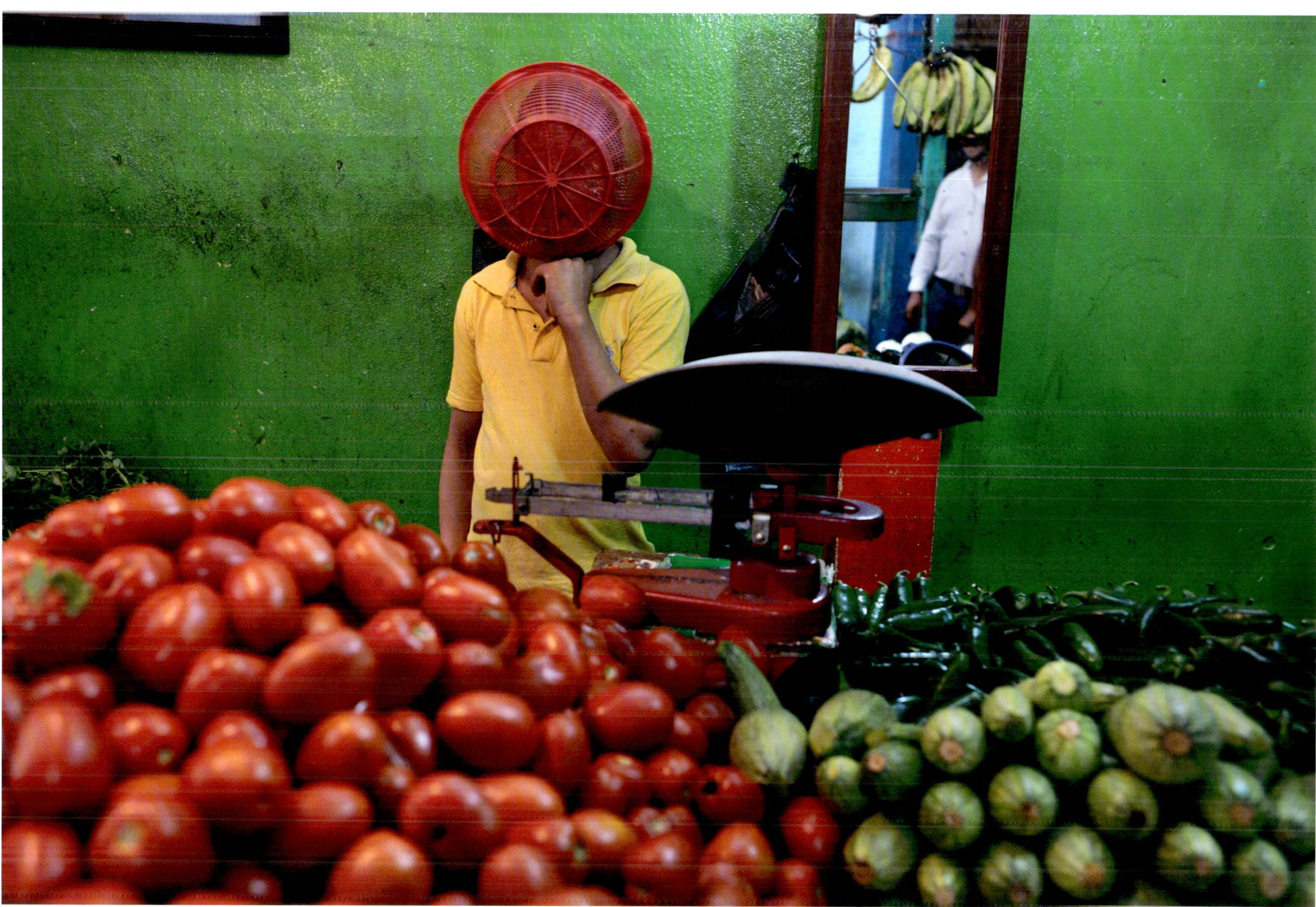

Las Vegas, 1997

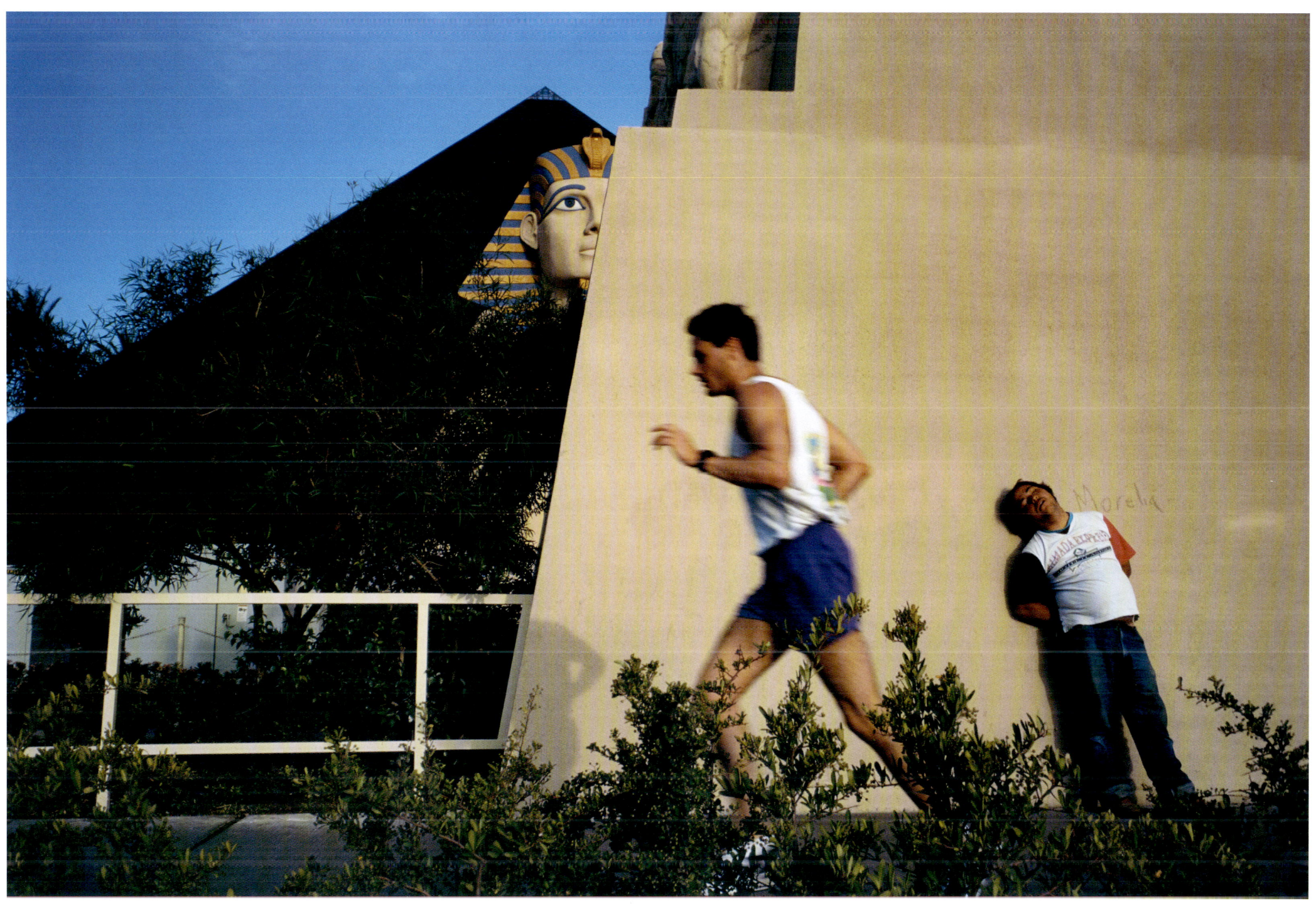

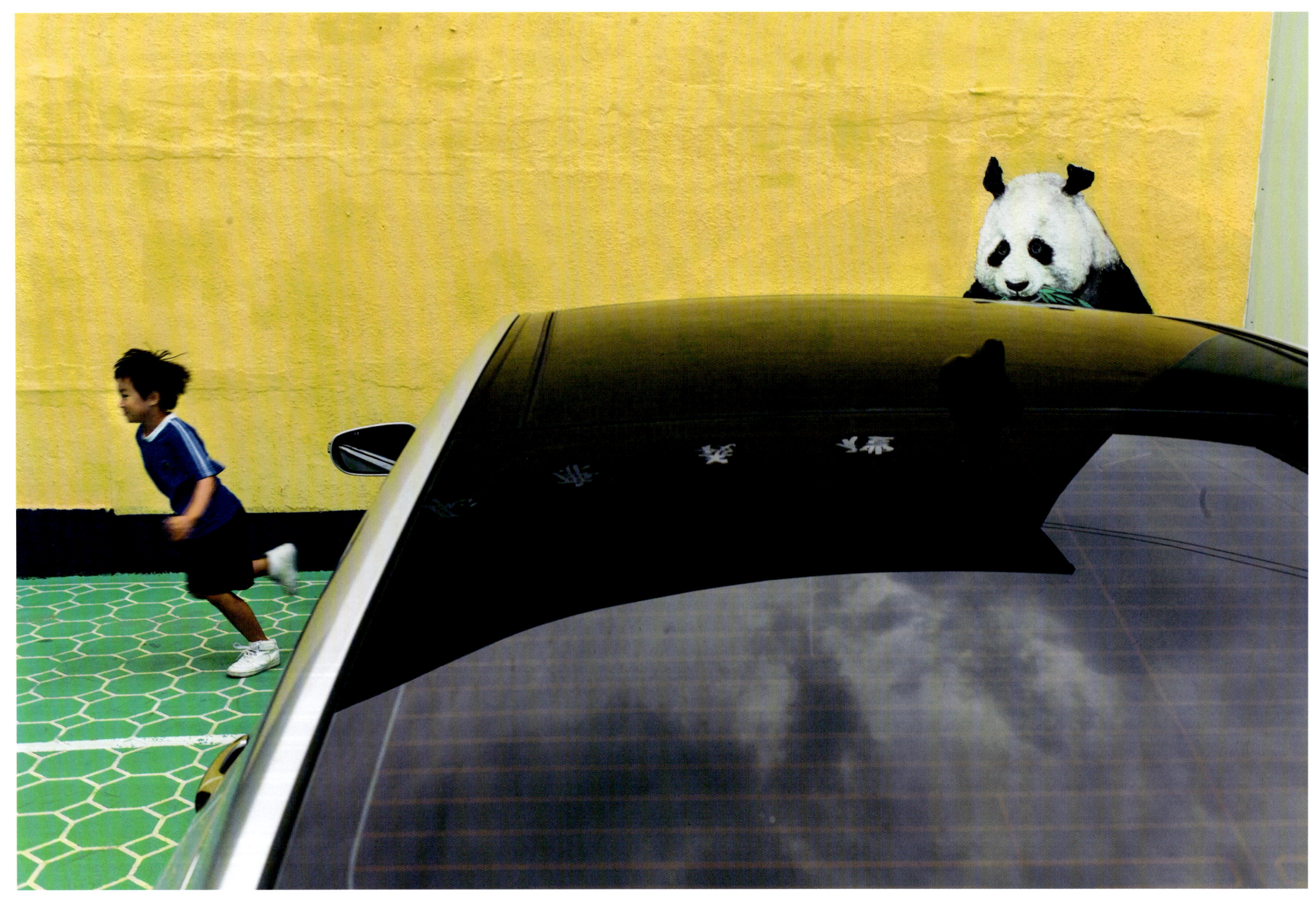

Daegu, South Korea, 2013

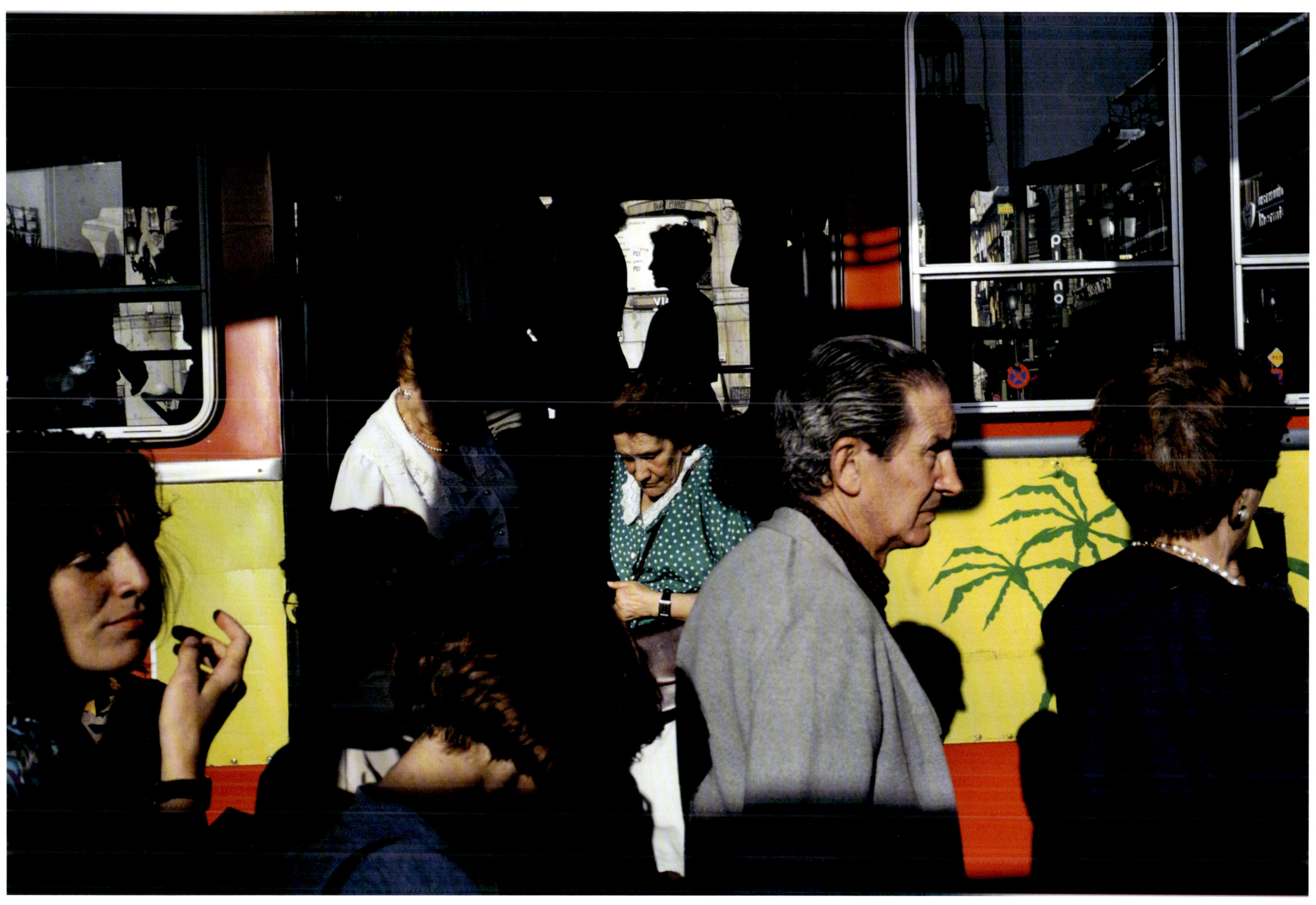

Madrid, 1992

Porto Cervo, Sardinia, 1998

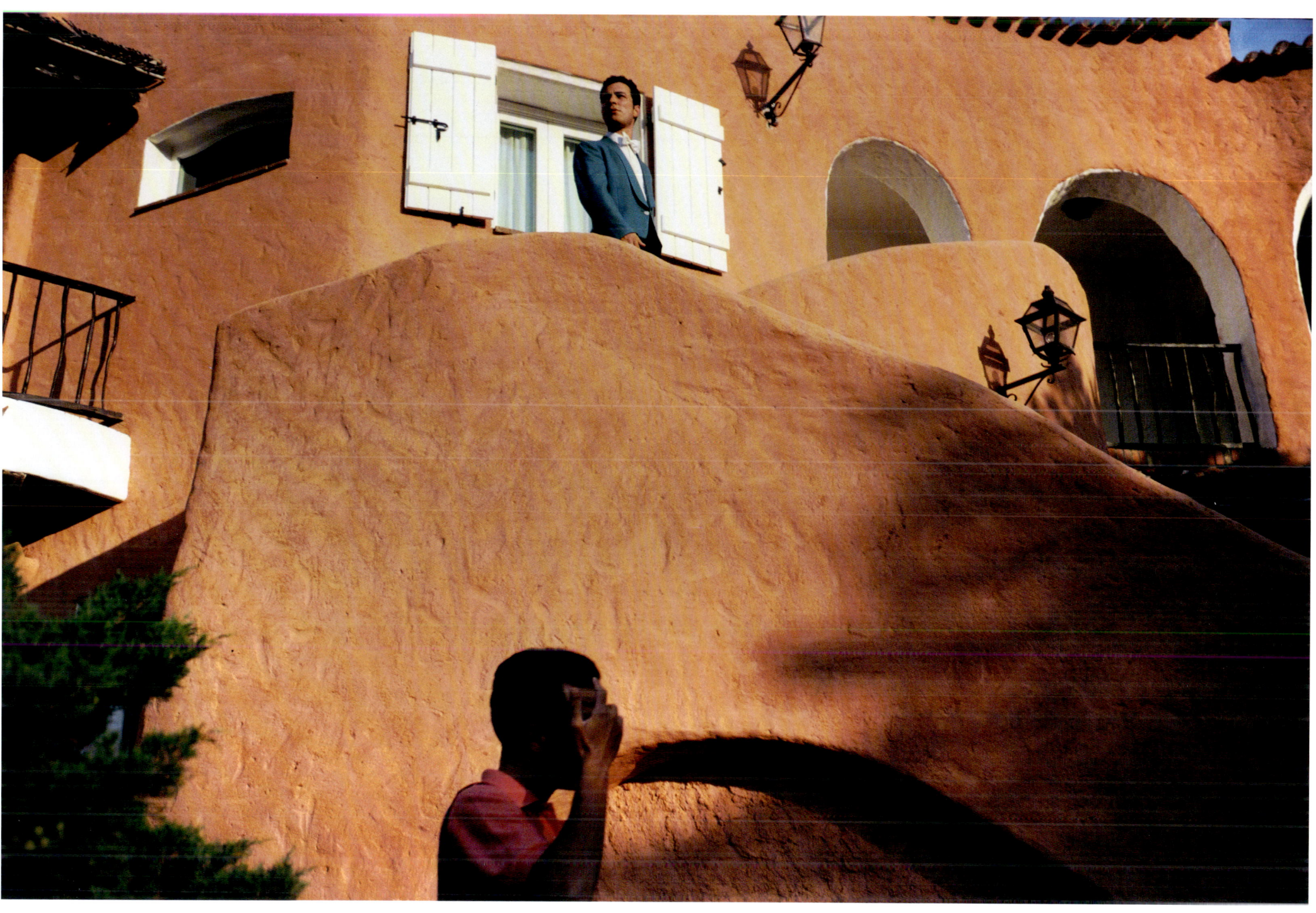

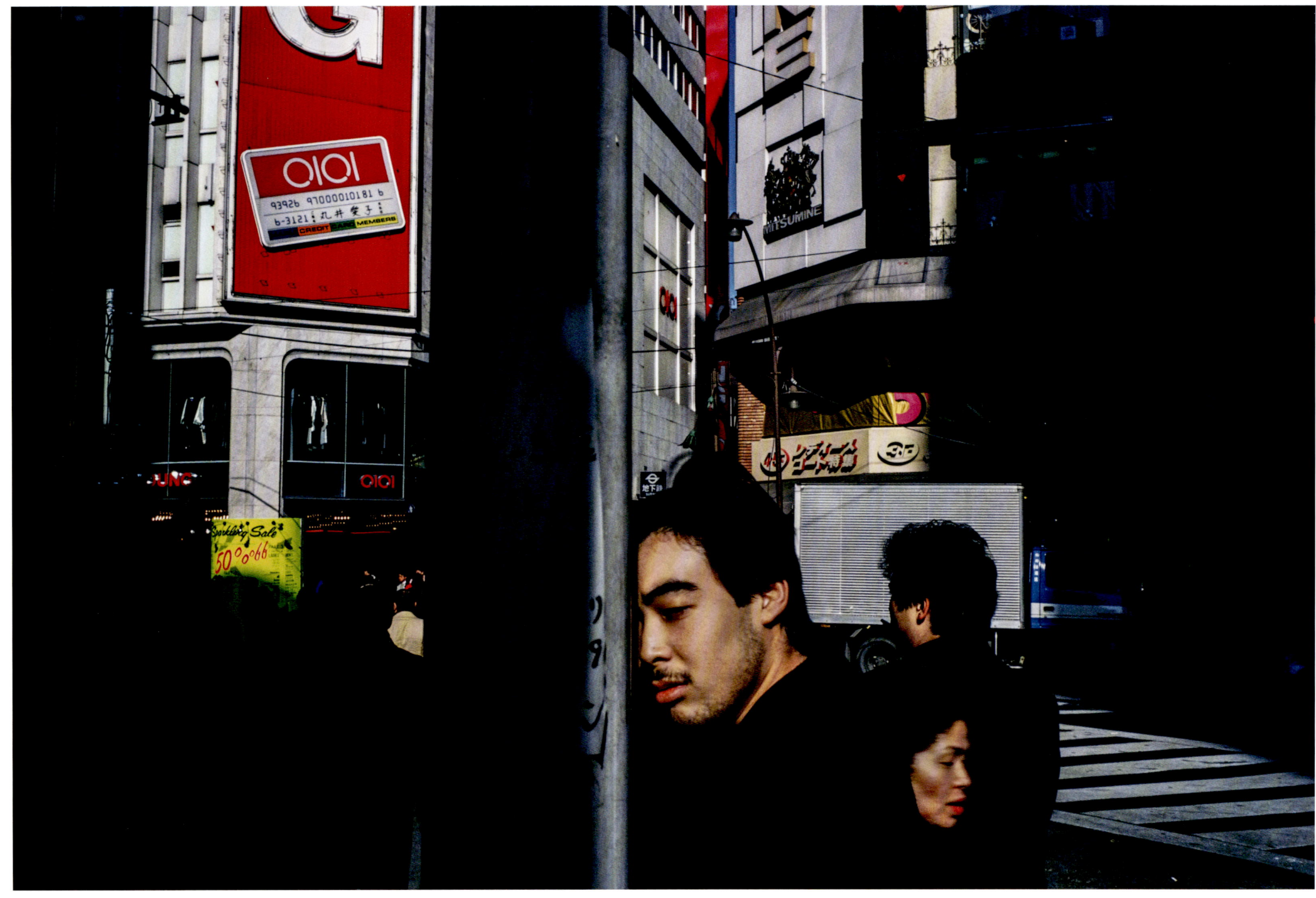

Tokyo, 1985

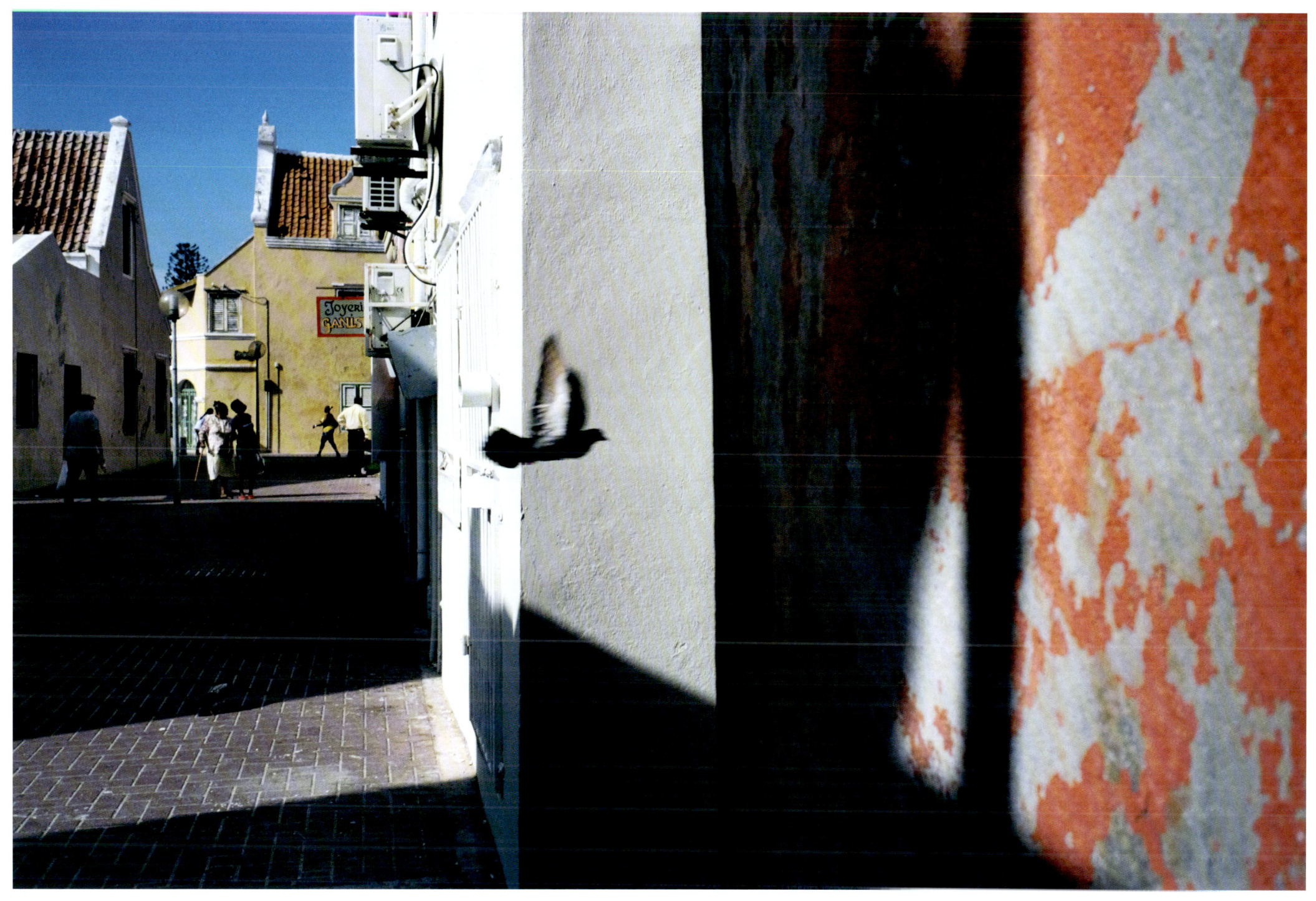

Willemstad, Curaçao, 2010

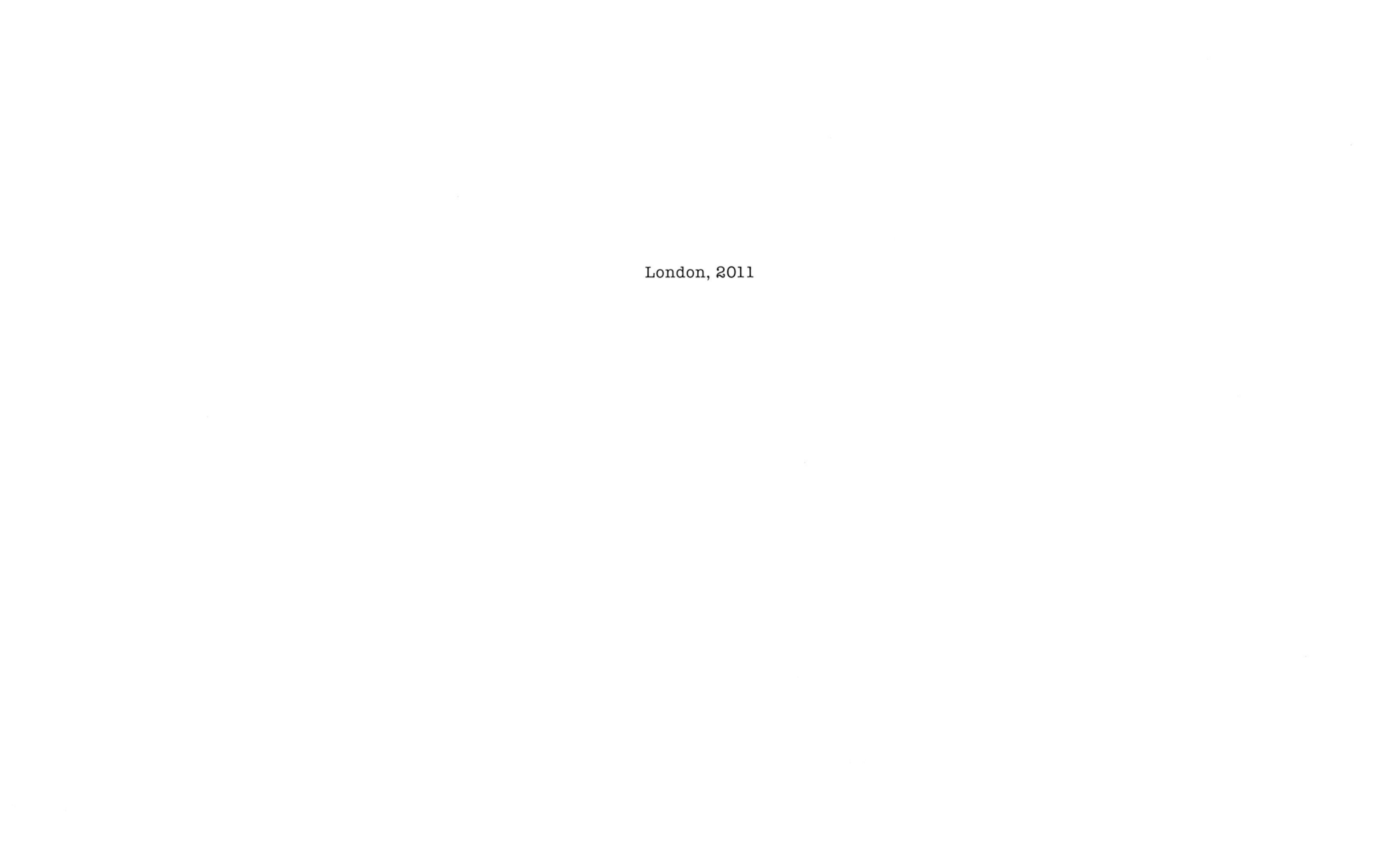

London, 2011

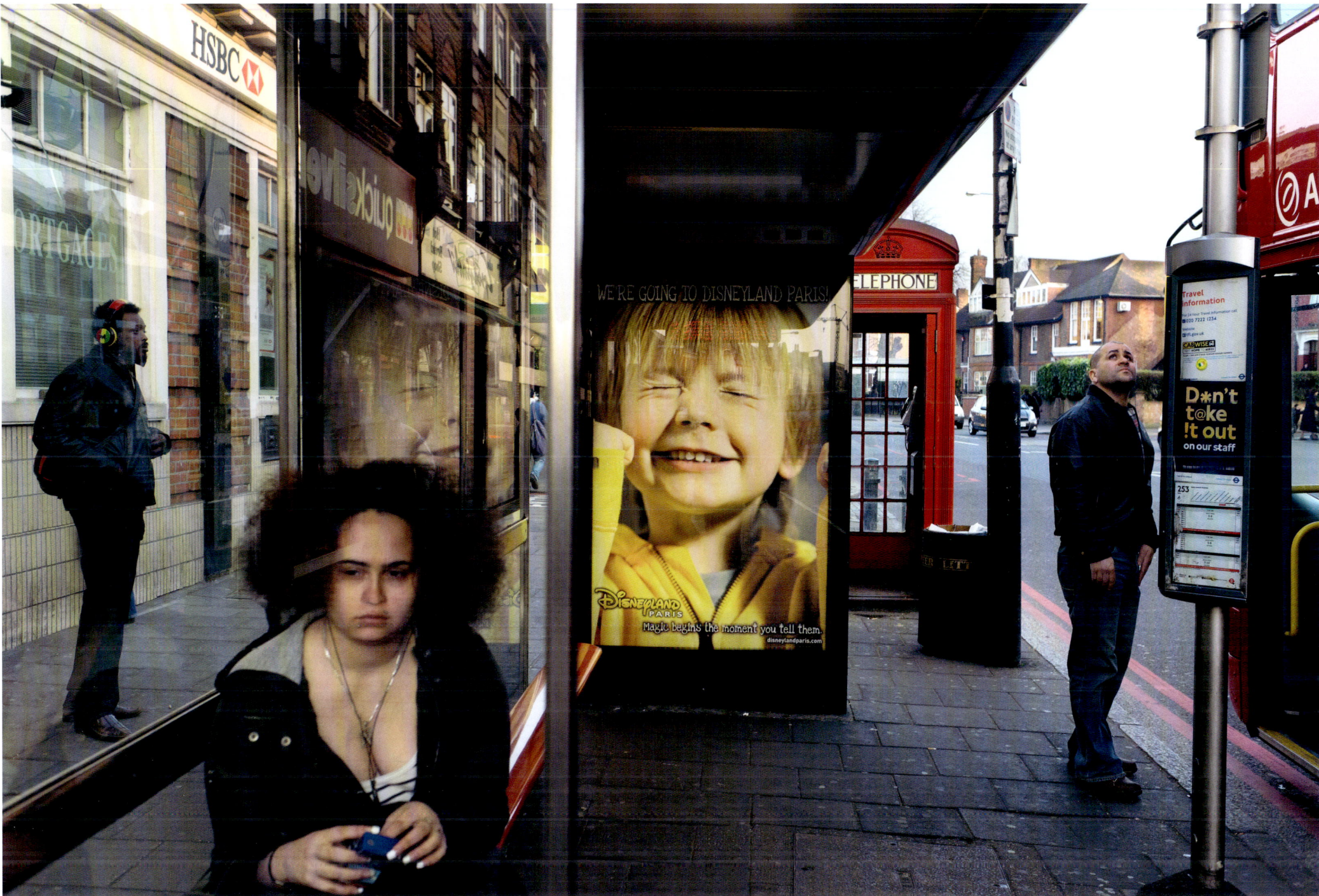

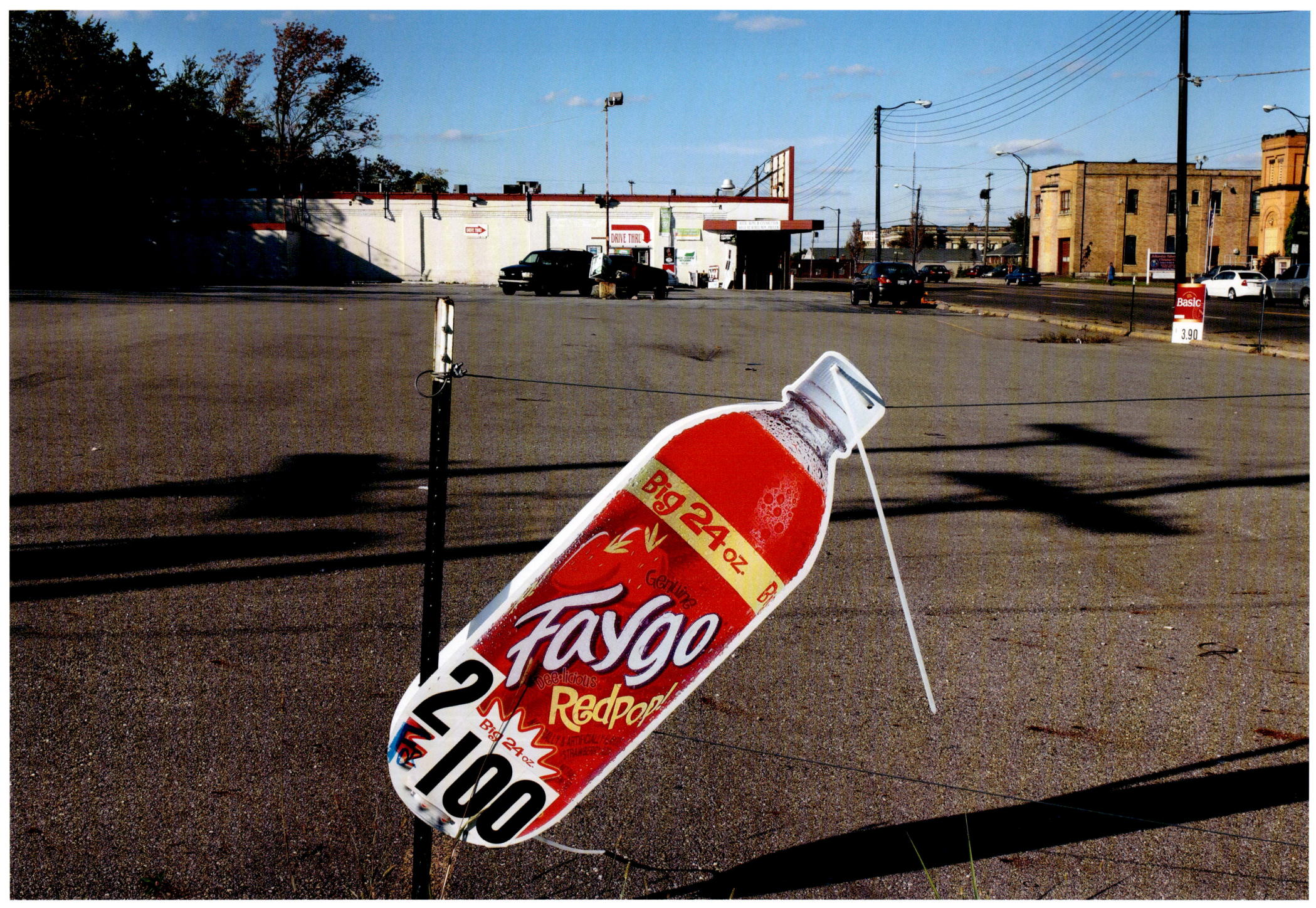

Youngstown, Ohio, 2008

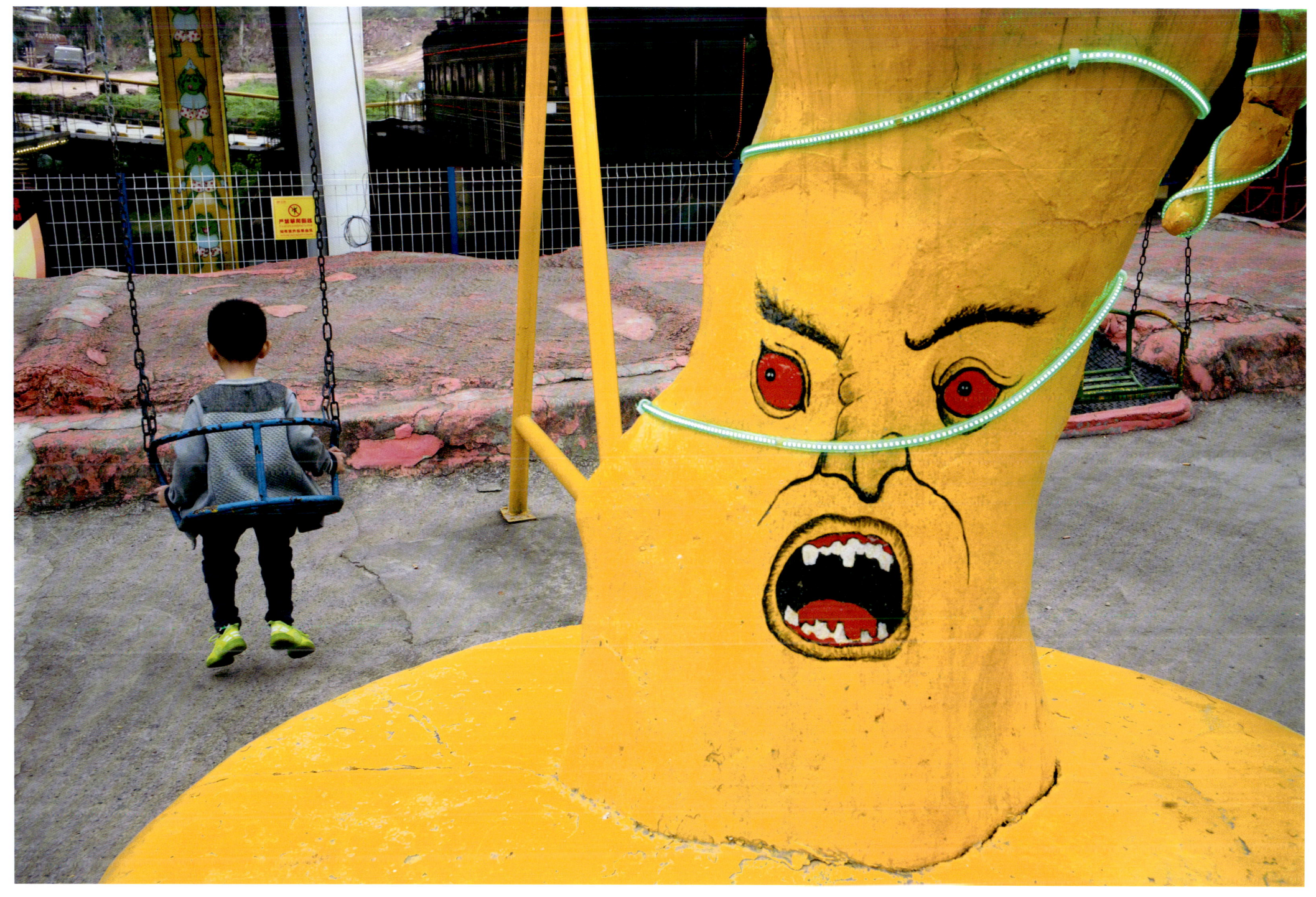

Chongqing, China, 2017

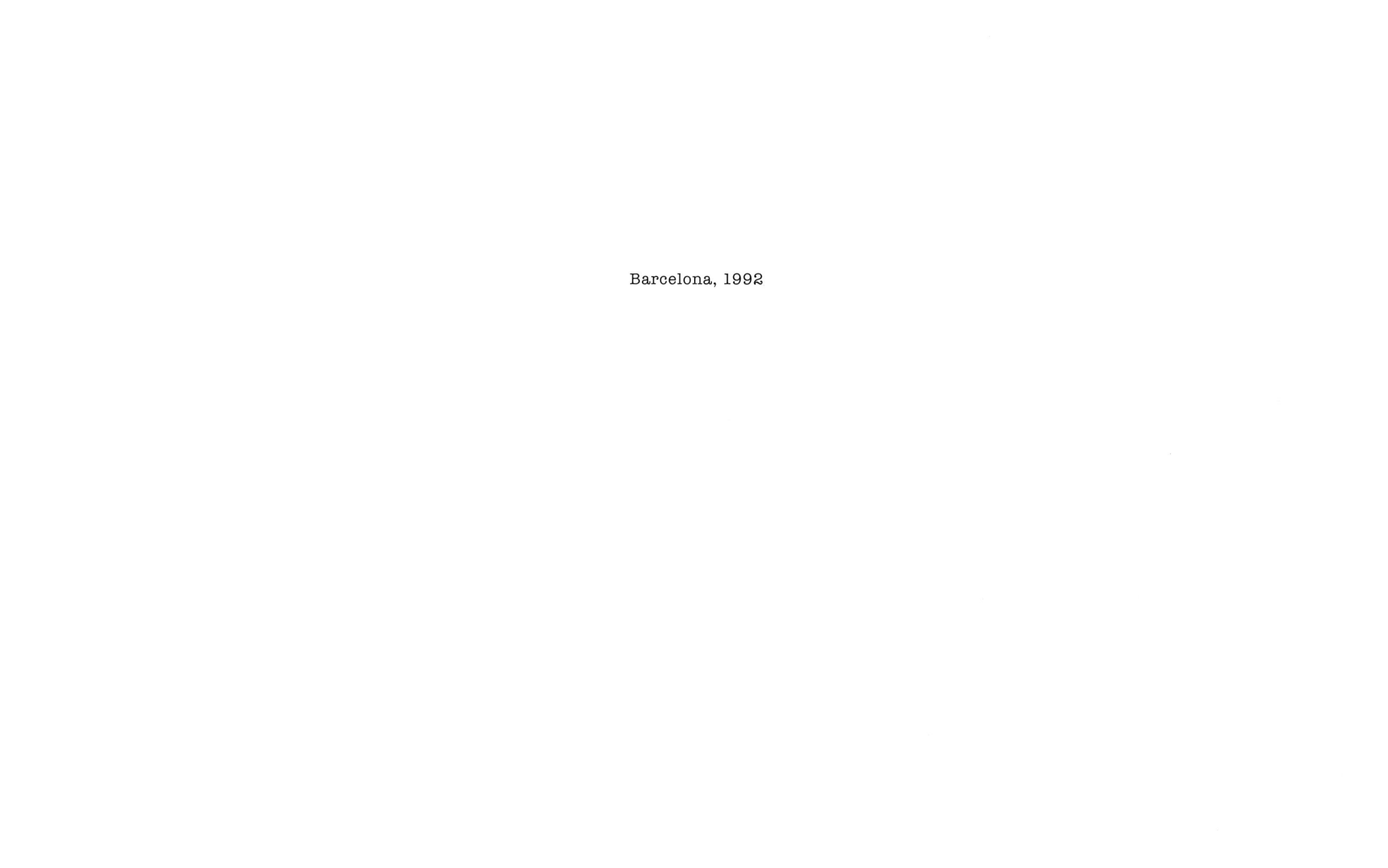

Barcelona, 1992

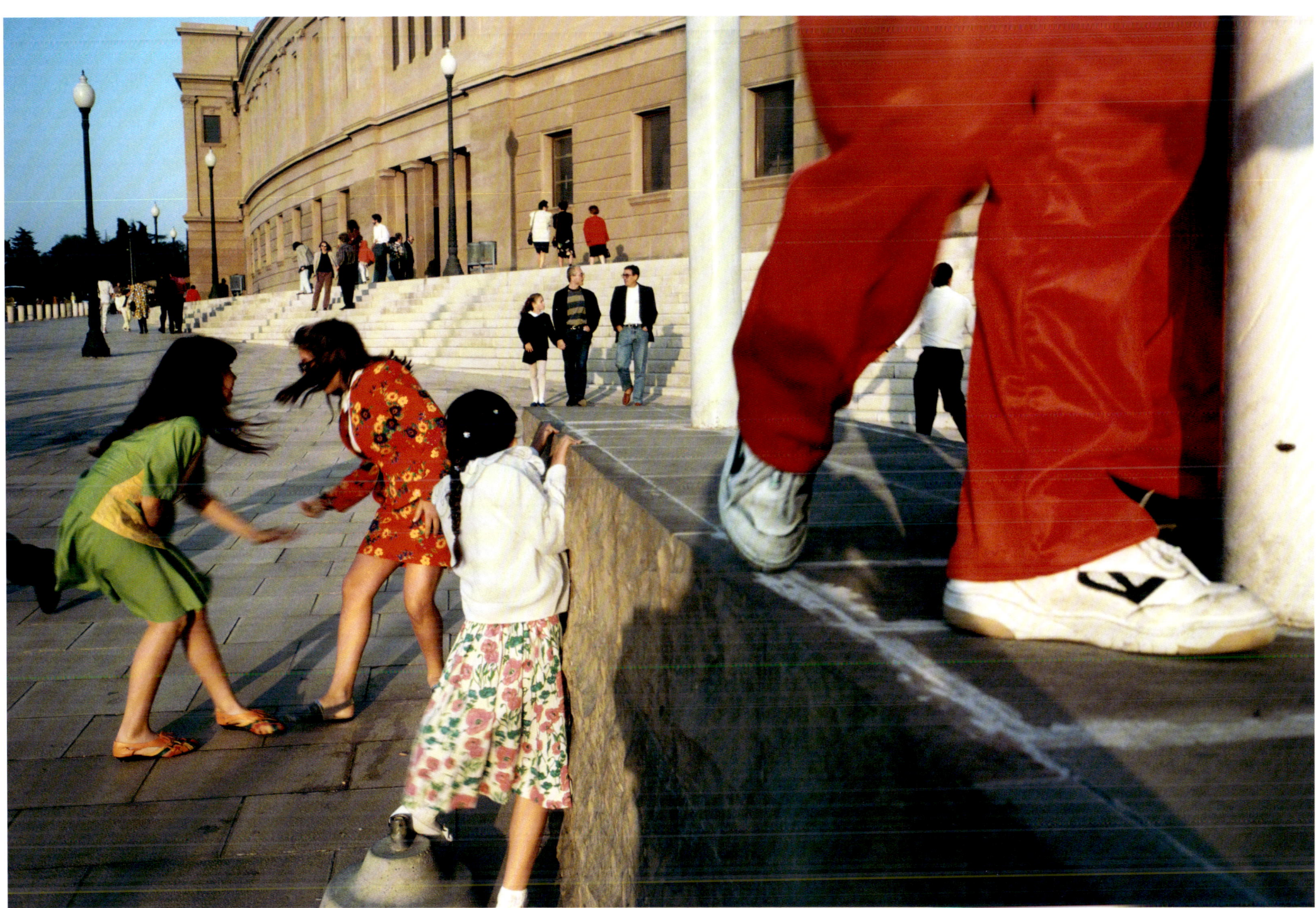

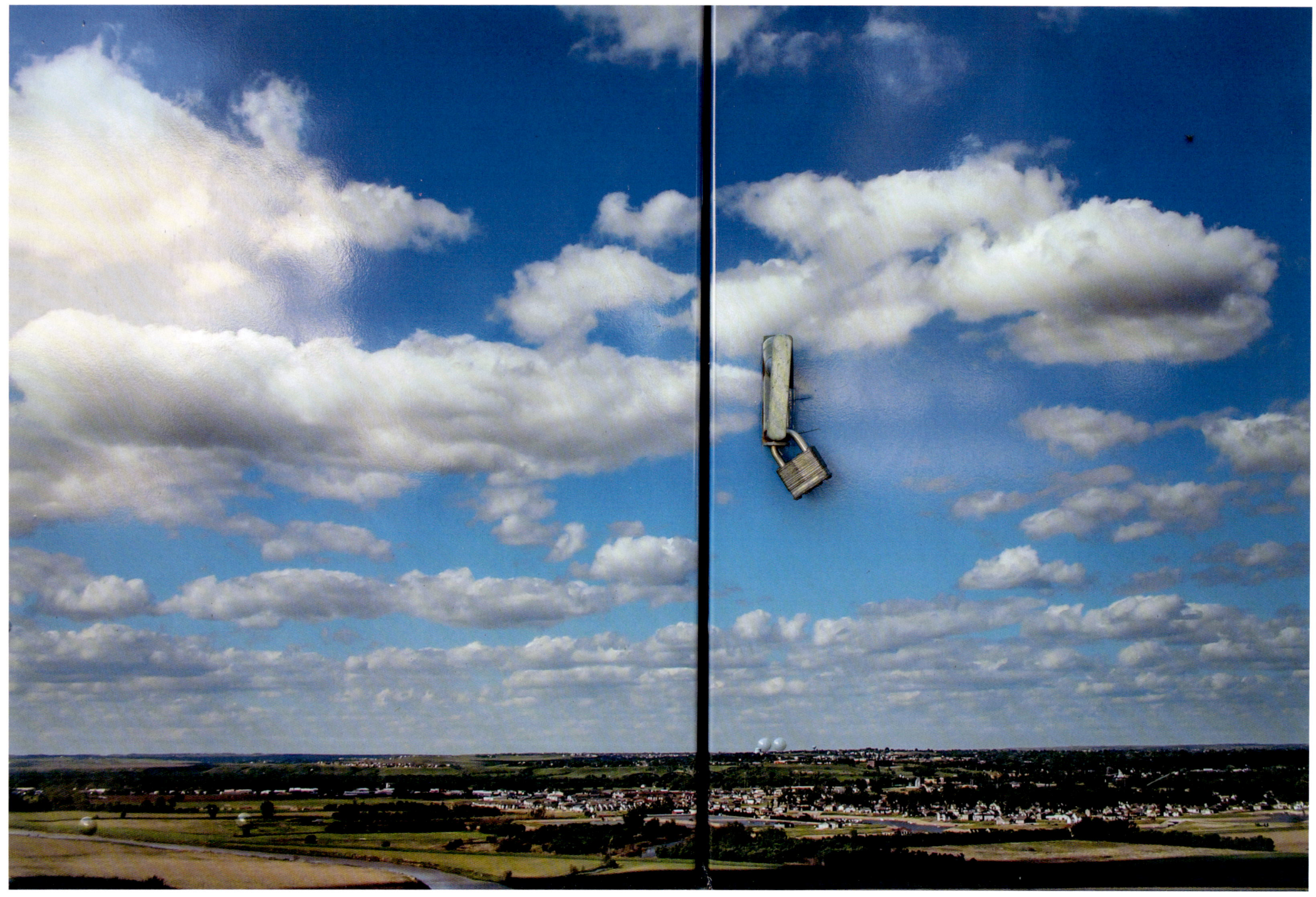

Bismarck, North Dakota, 2019

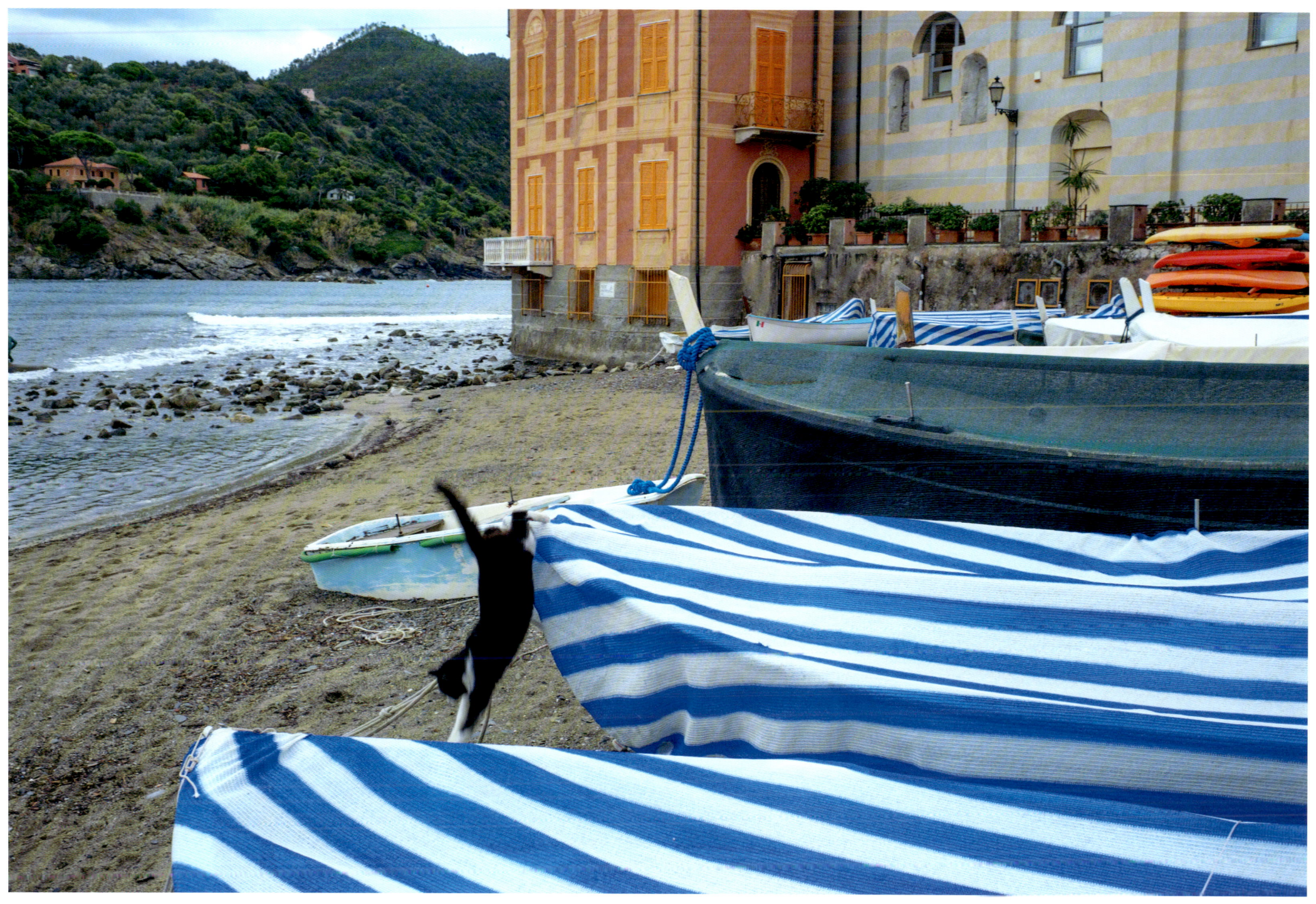

Sestri Levante, Italy, 2015

Coney Island, New York, 2016

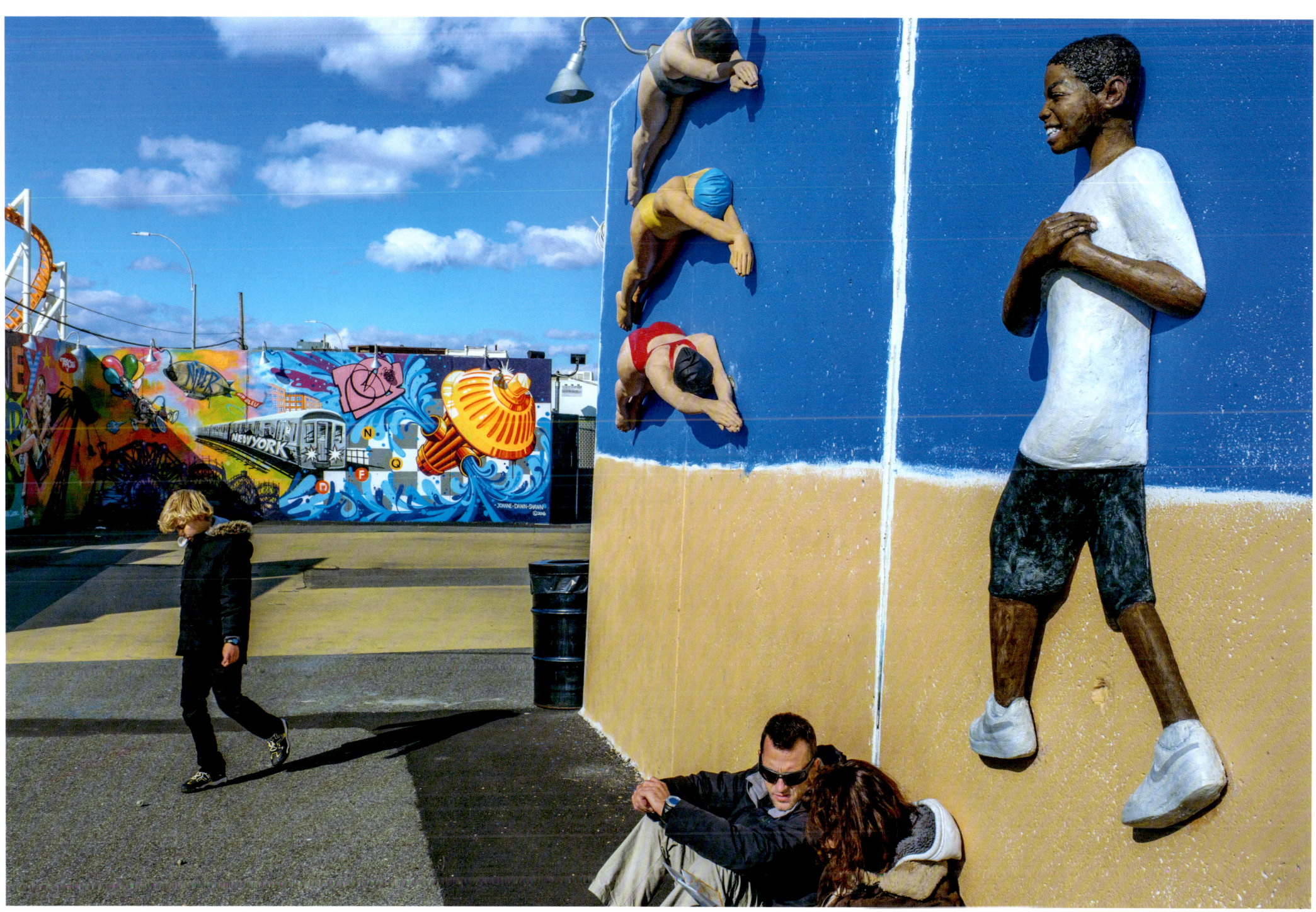

Milan, 2016

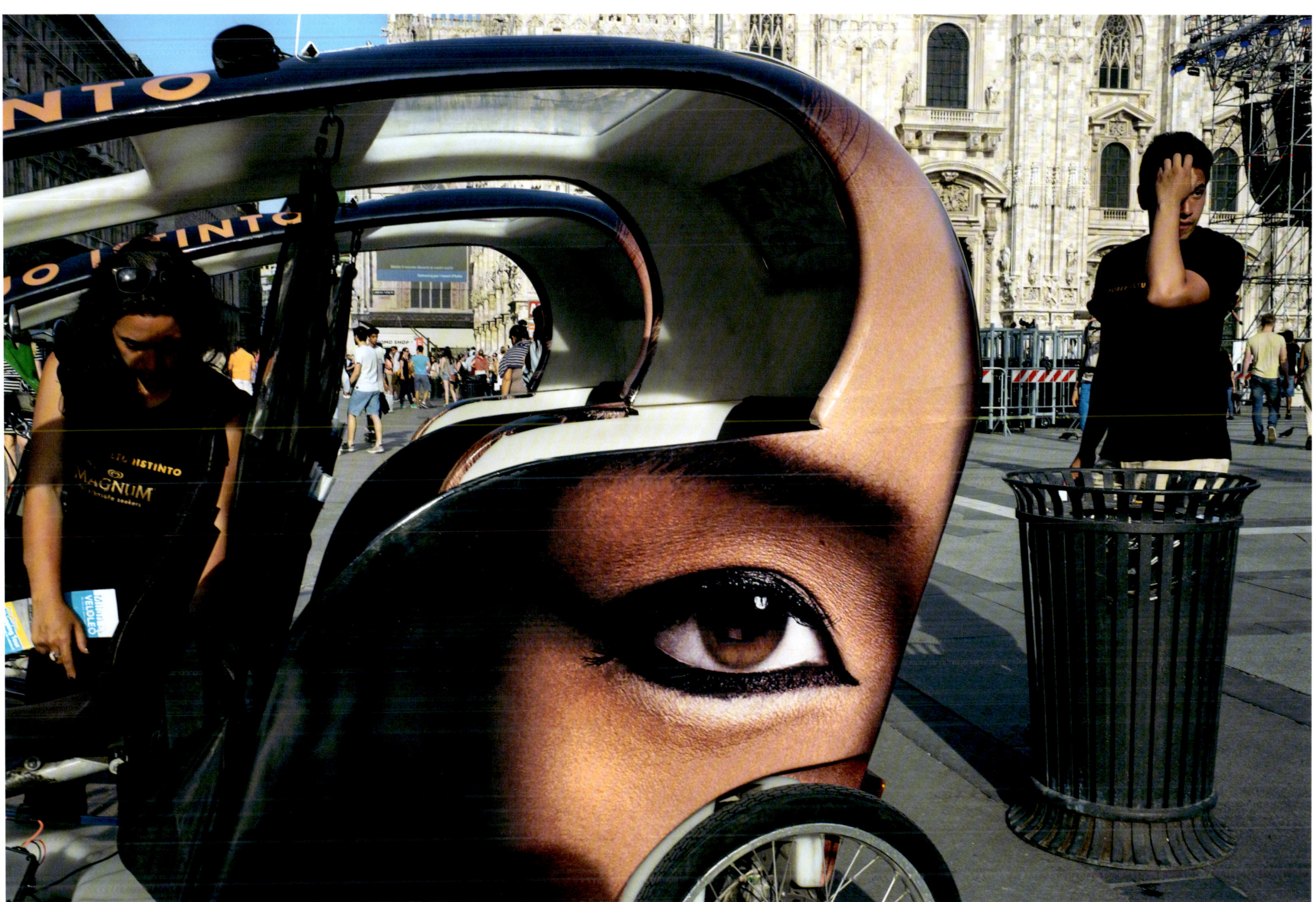

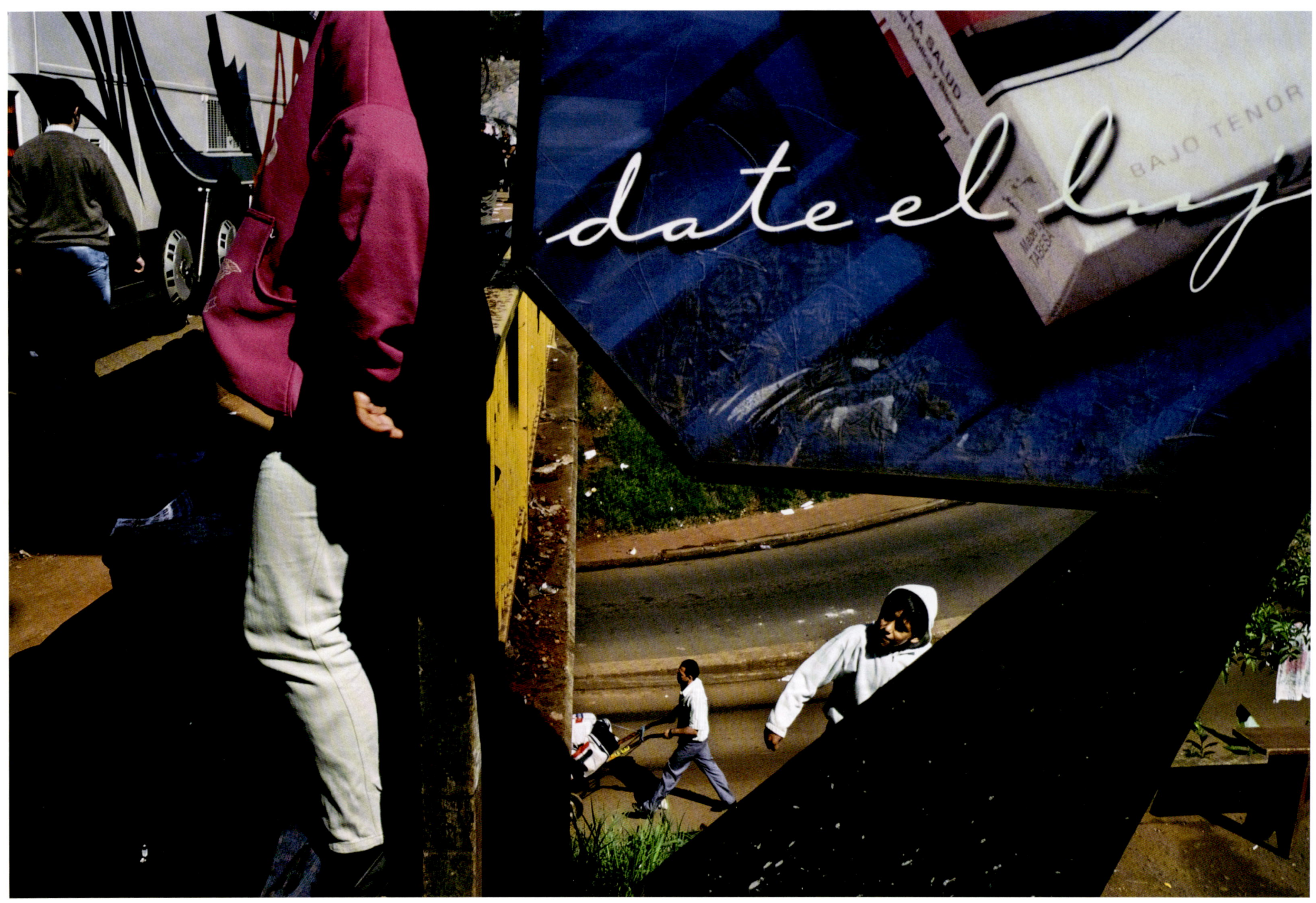

Ciudad del Este, Paraguay, 1998

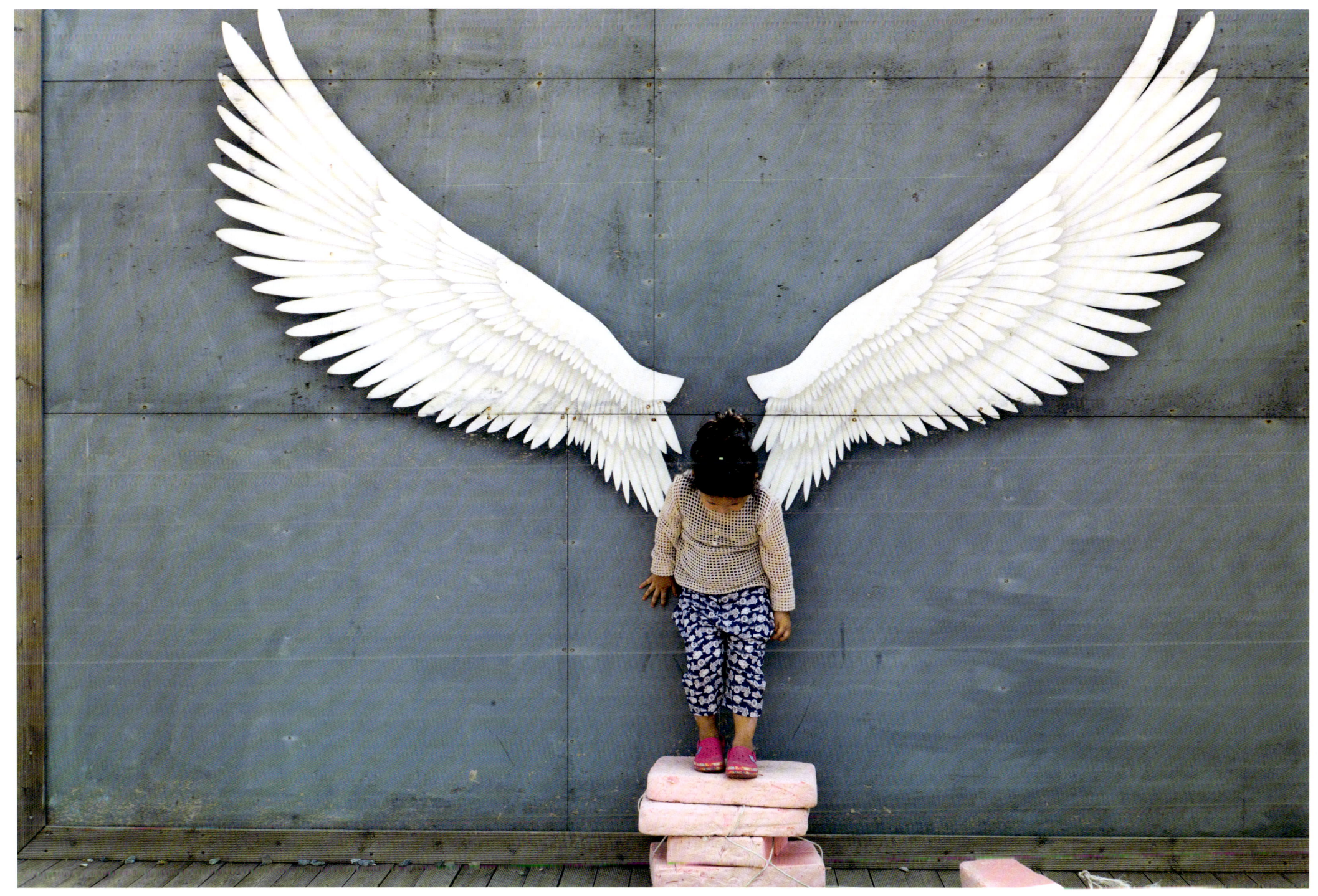

Jeongseon, South Korea, 2013

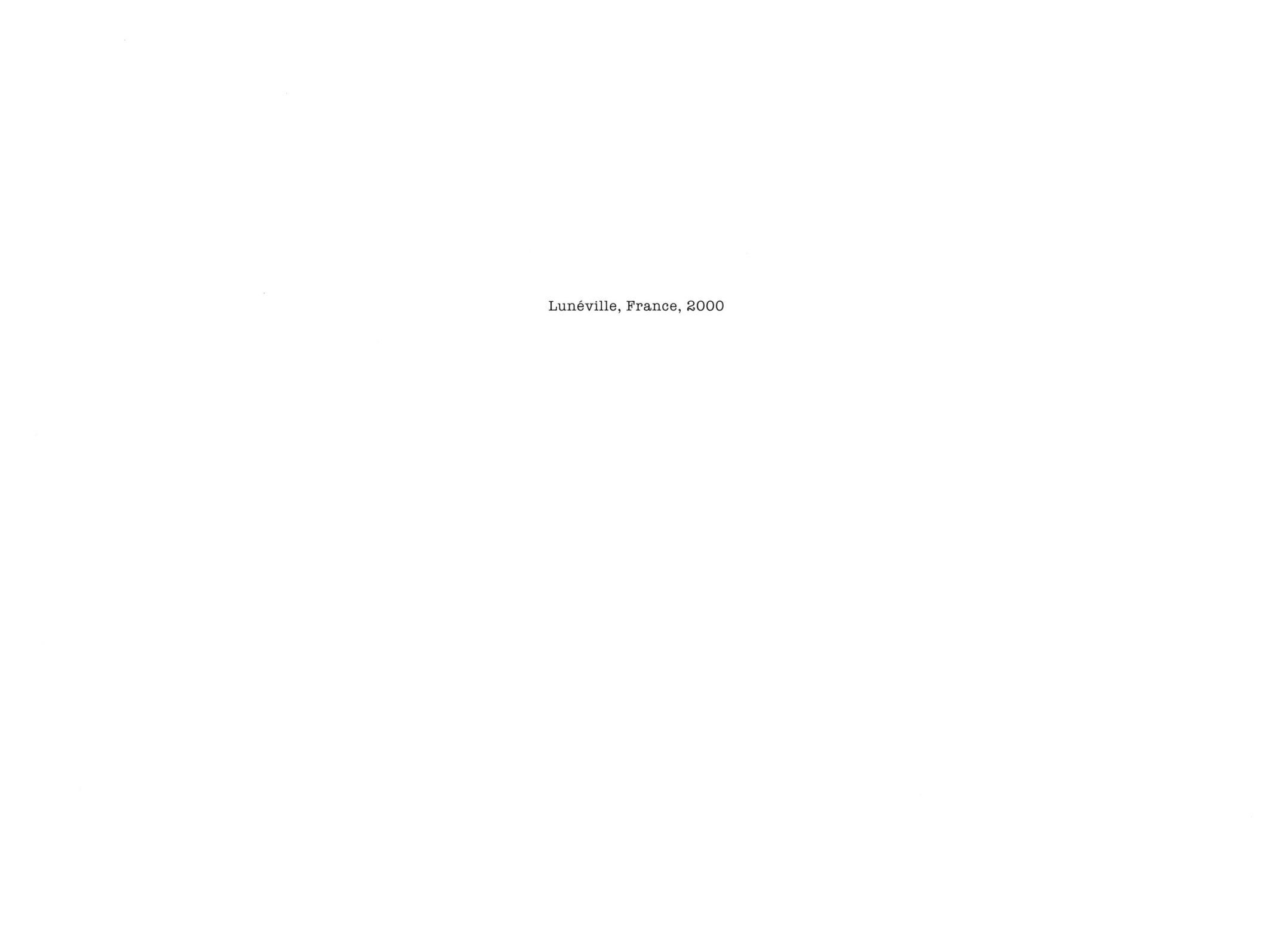

Lunéville, France, 2000

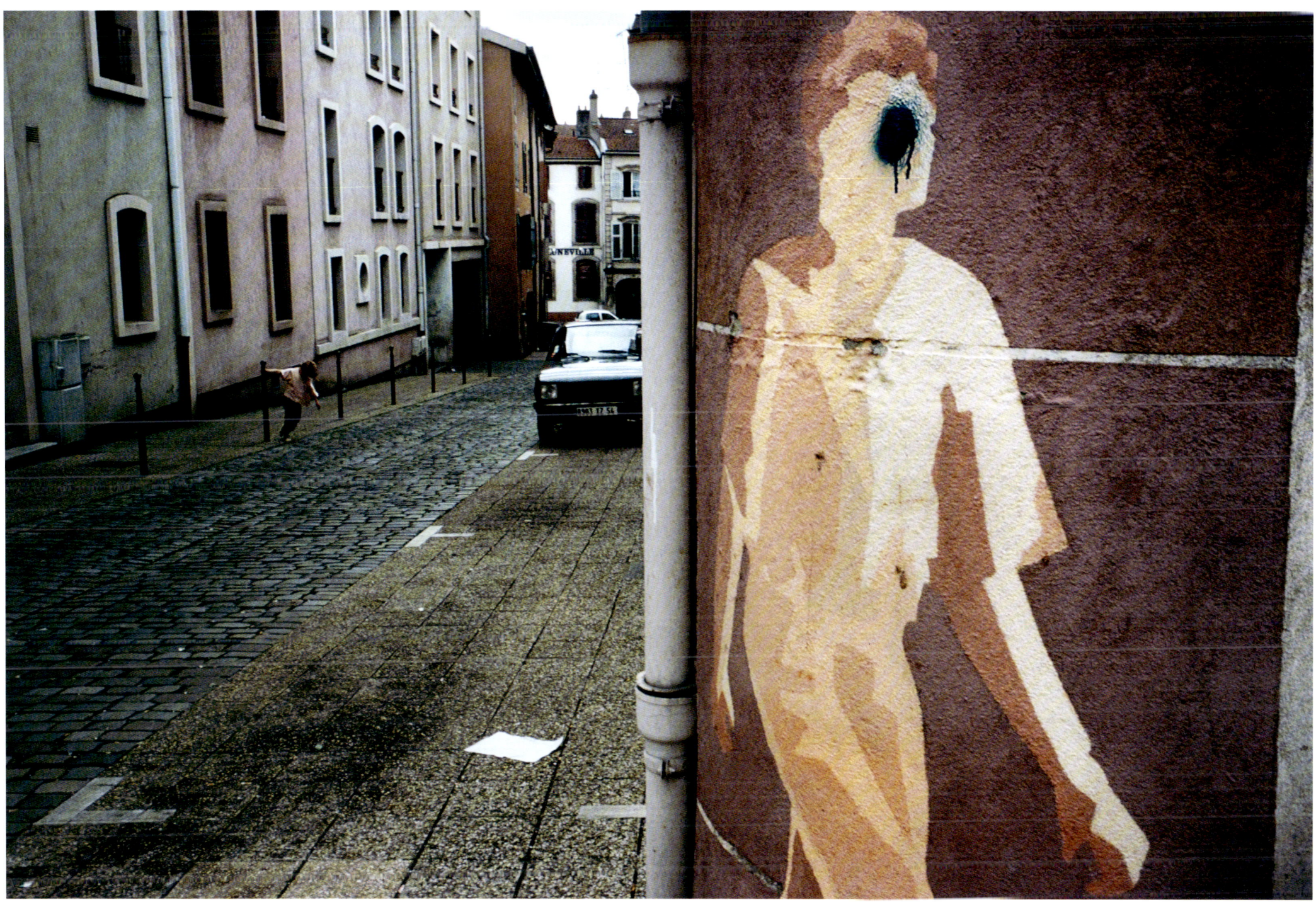

Buffalo, New York, 2017

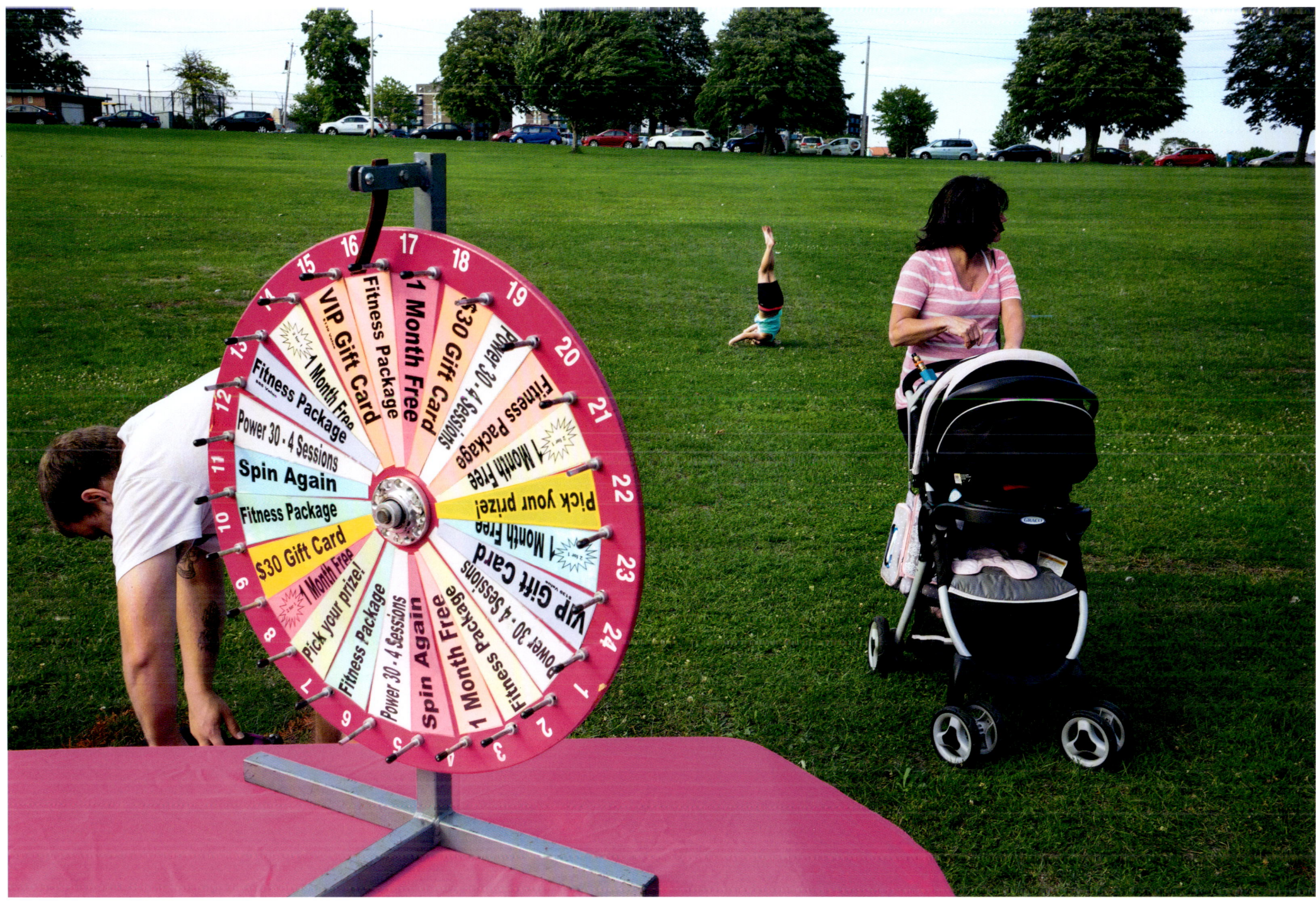

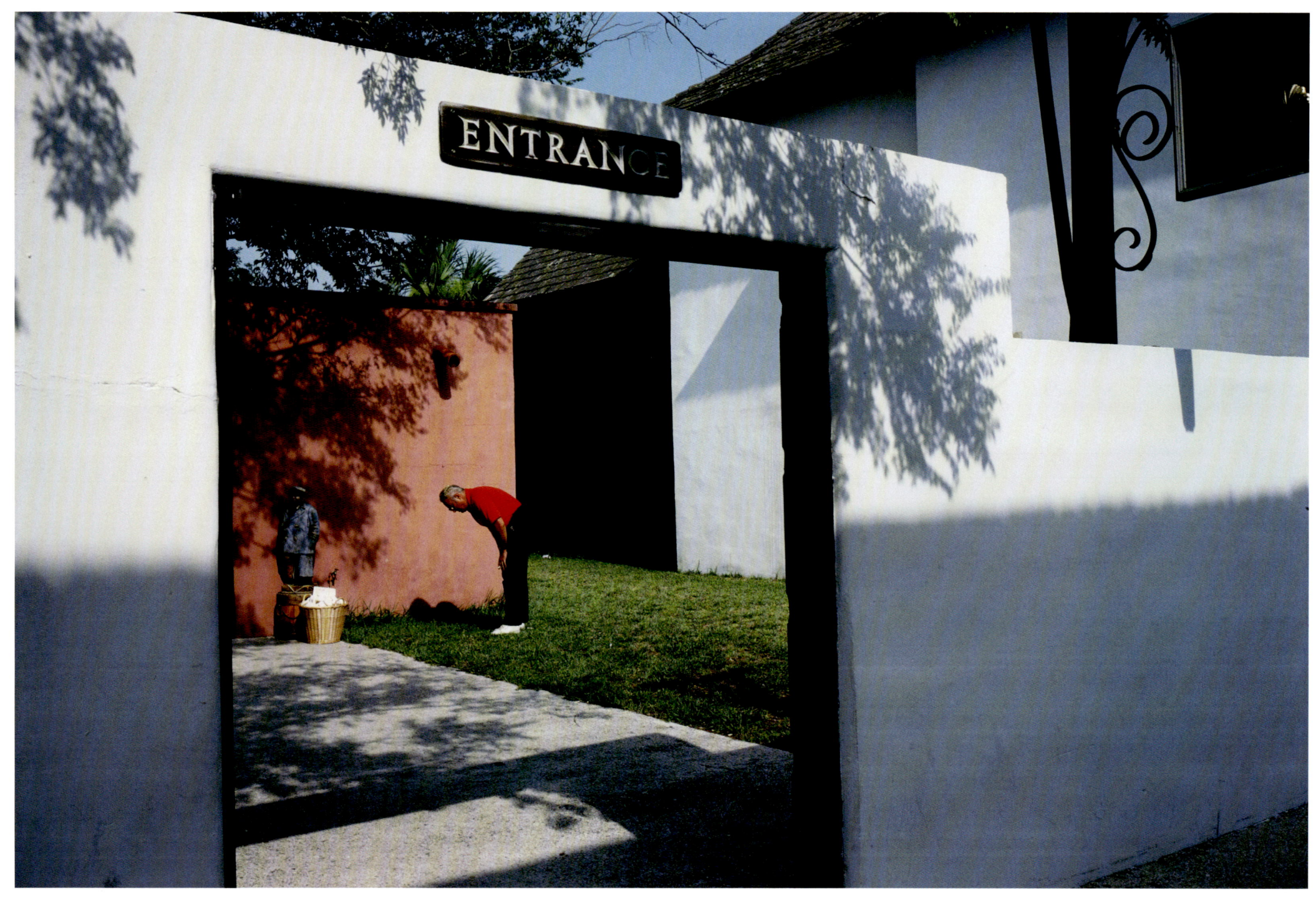

St. Augustine, Florida, 1989

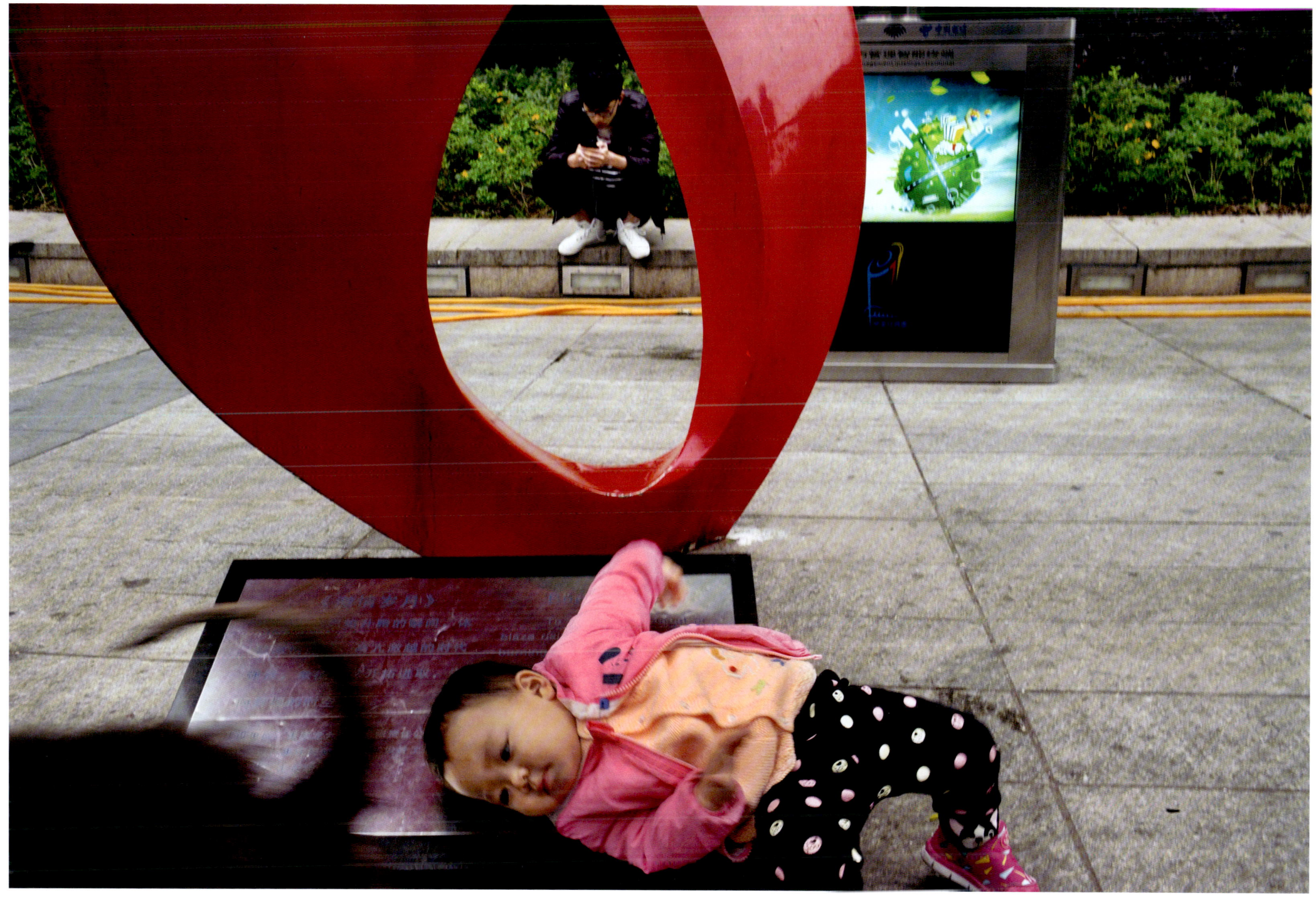

Chongqing, China, 2017

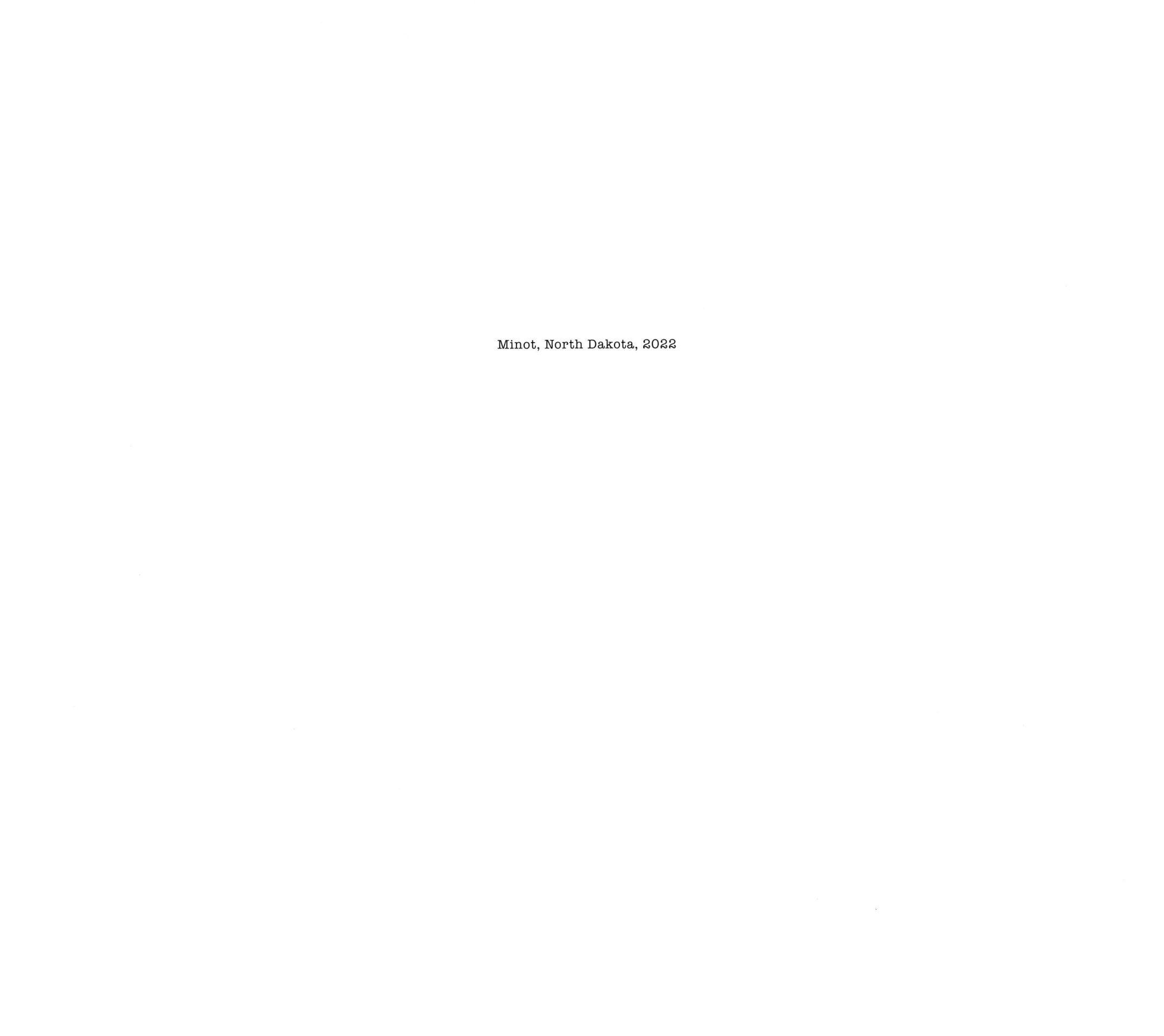

Minot, North Dakota, 2022

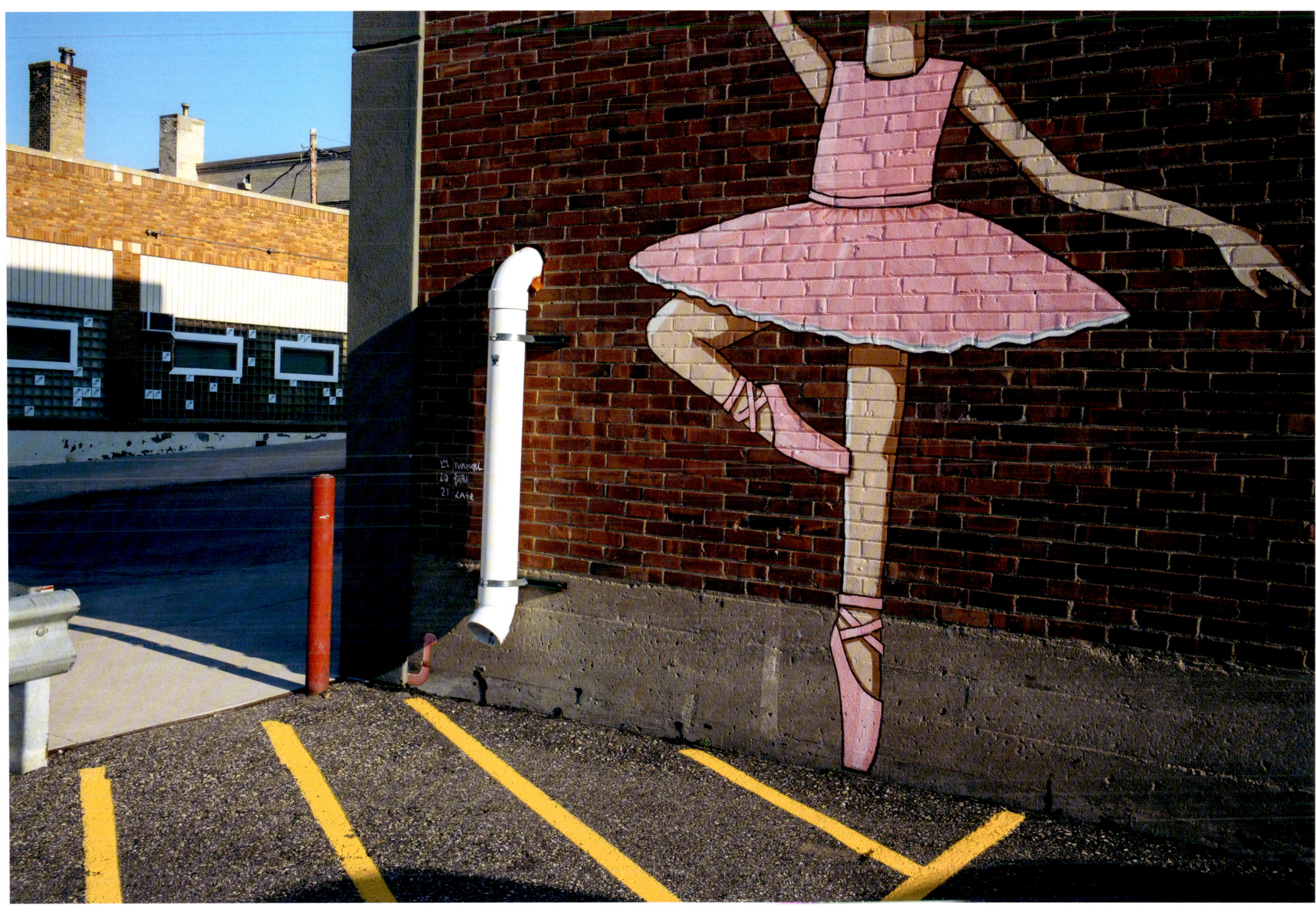

Rapid City, South Dakota, 2022

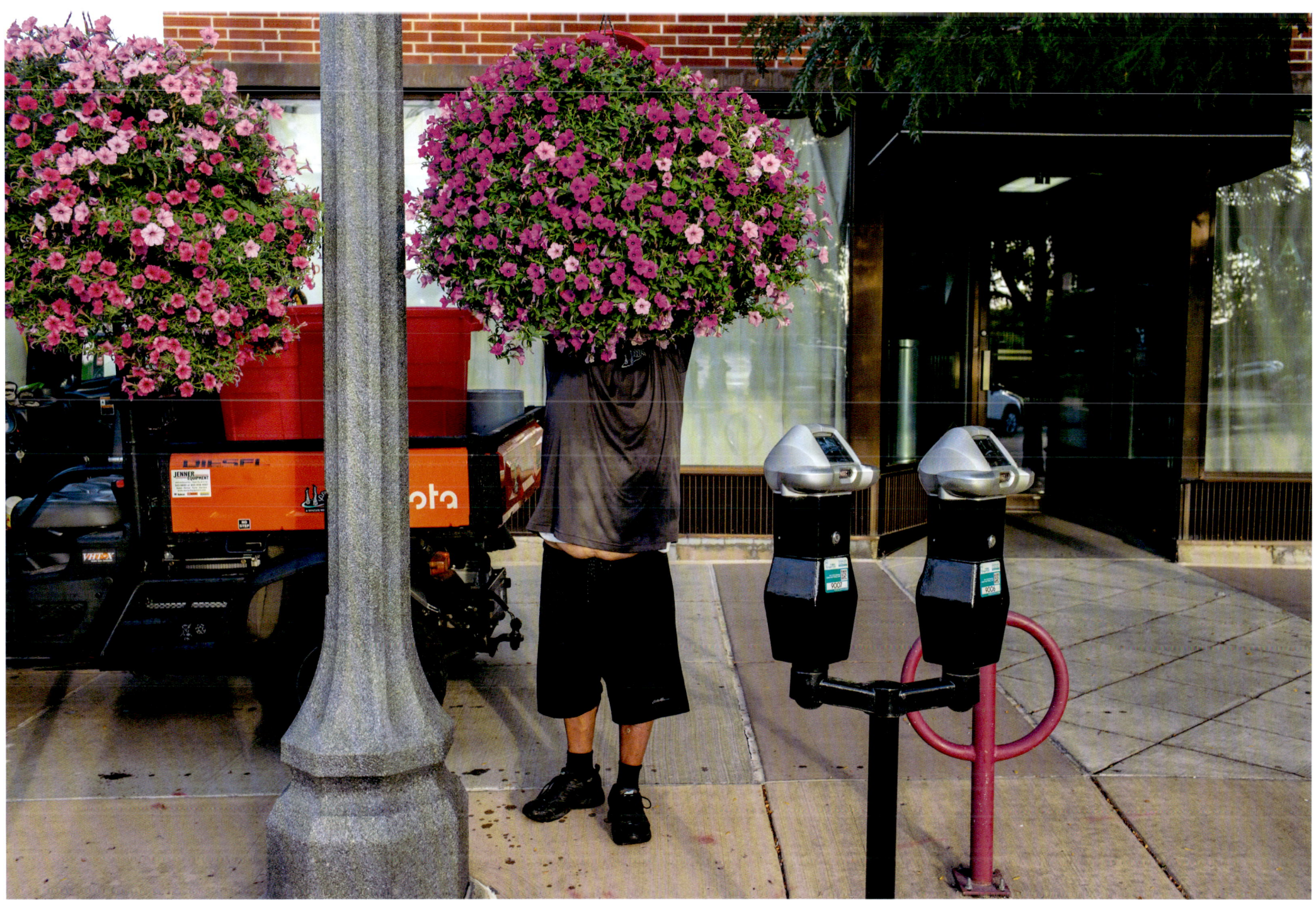

Coney Island, New York, 1983

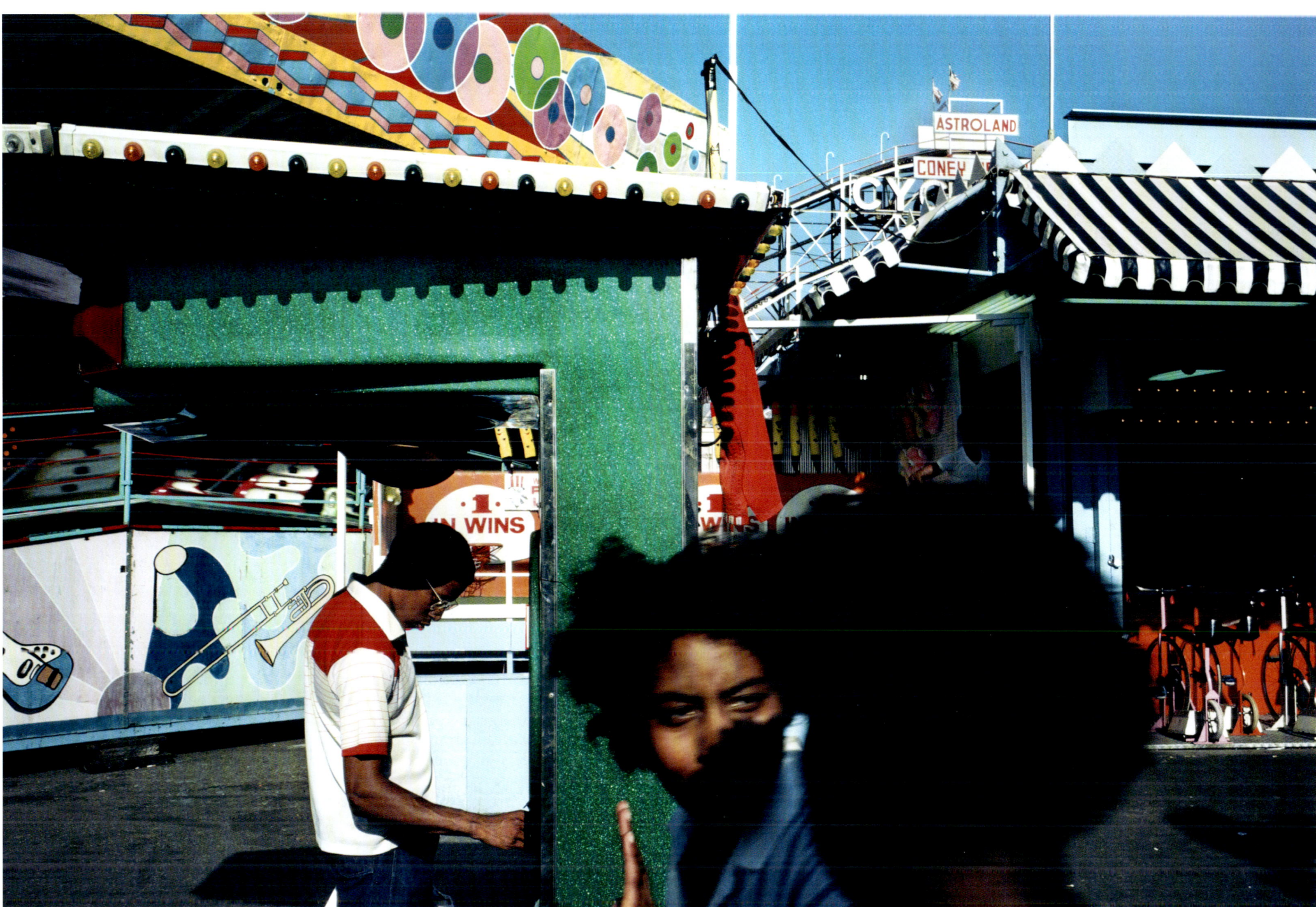

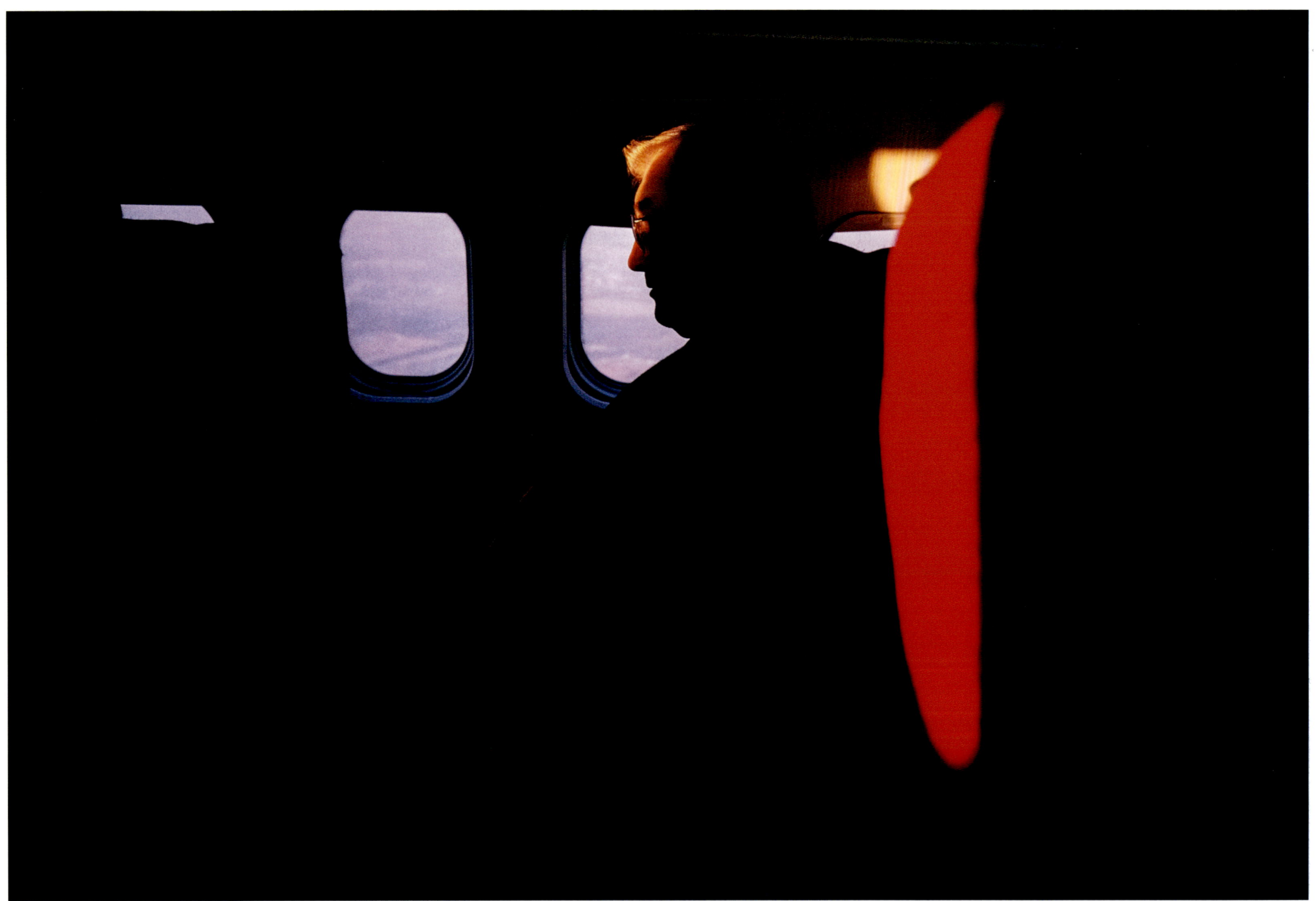

Above Ohio, 1983

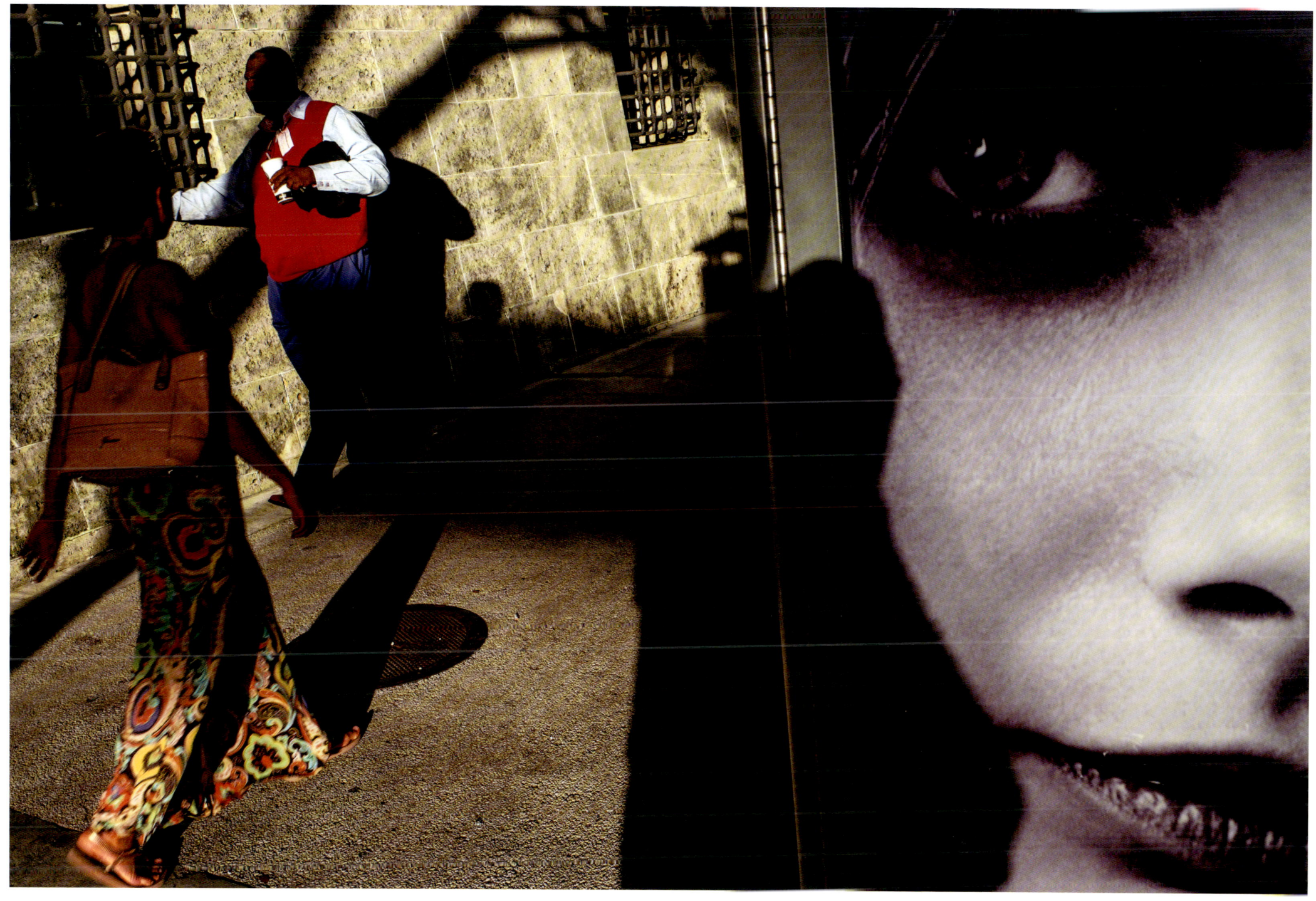

Miami, 2014

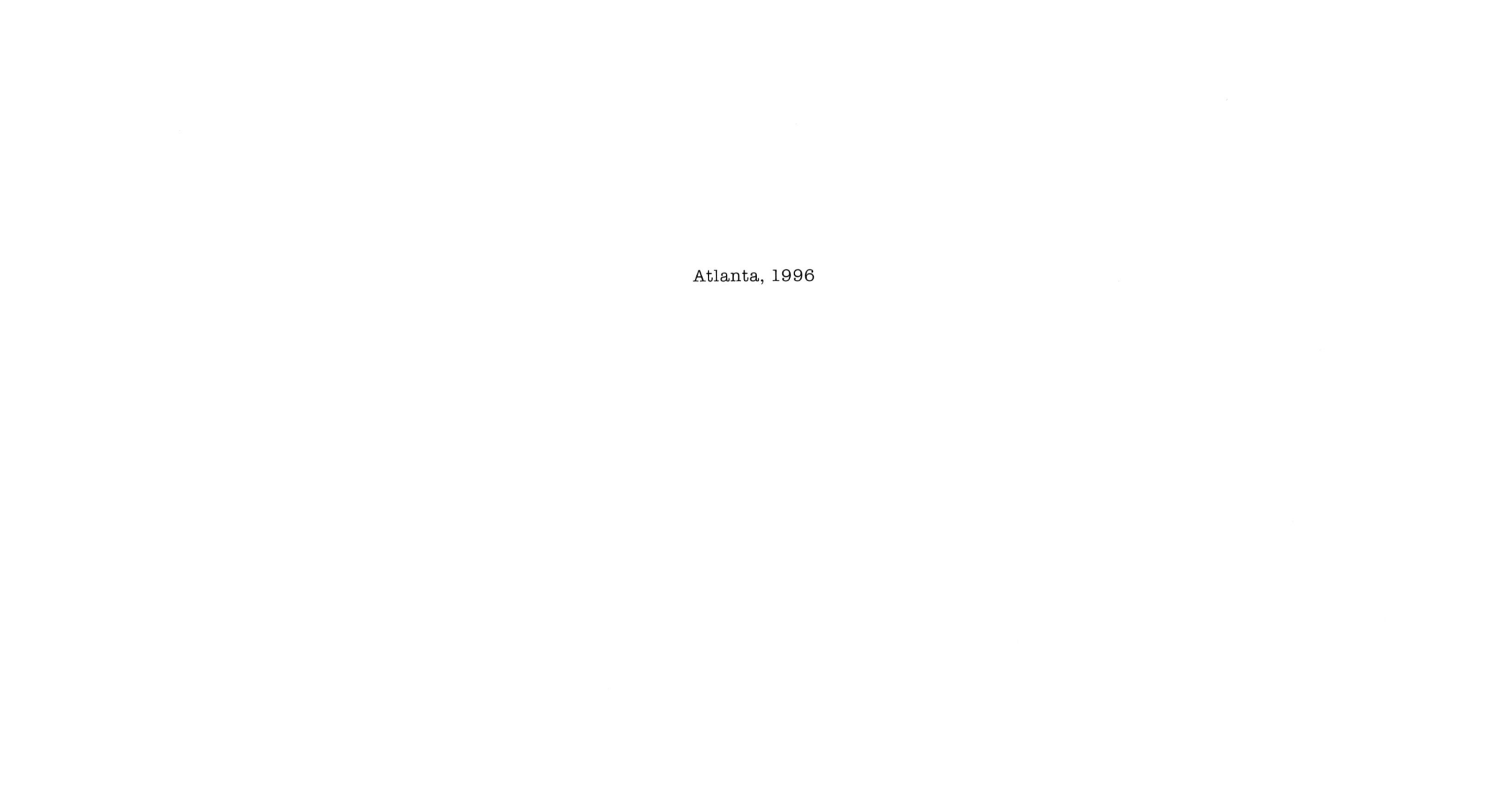

Atlanta, 1996

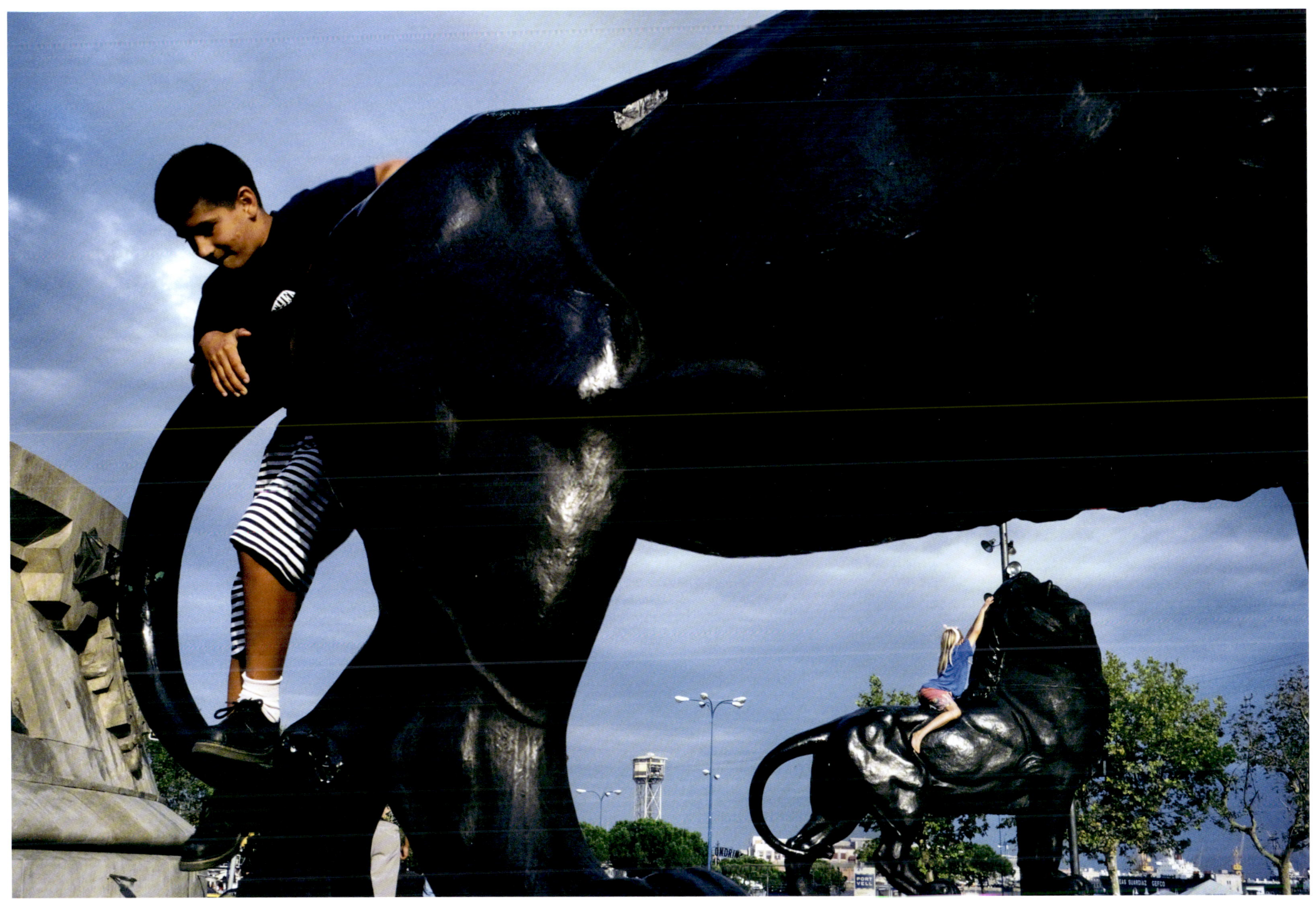

Barcelona, 1992

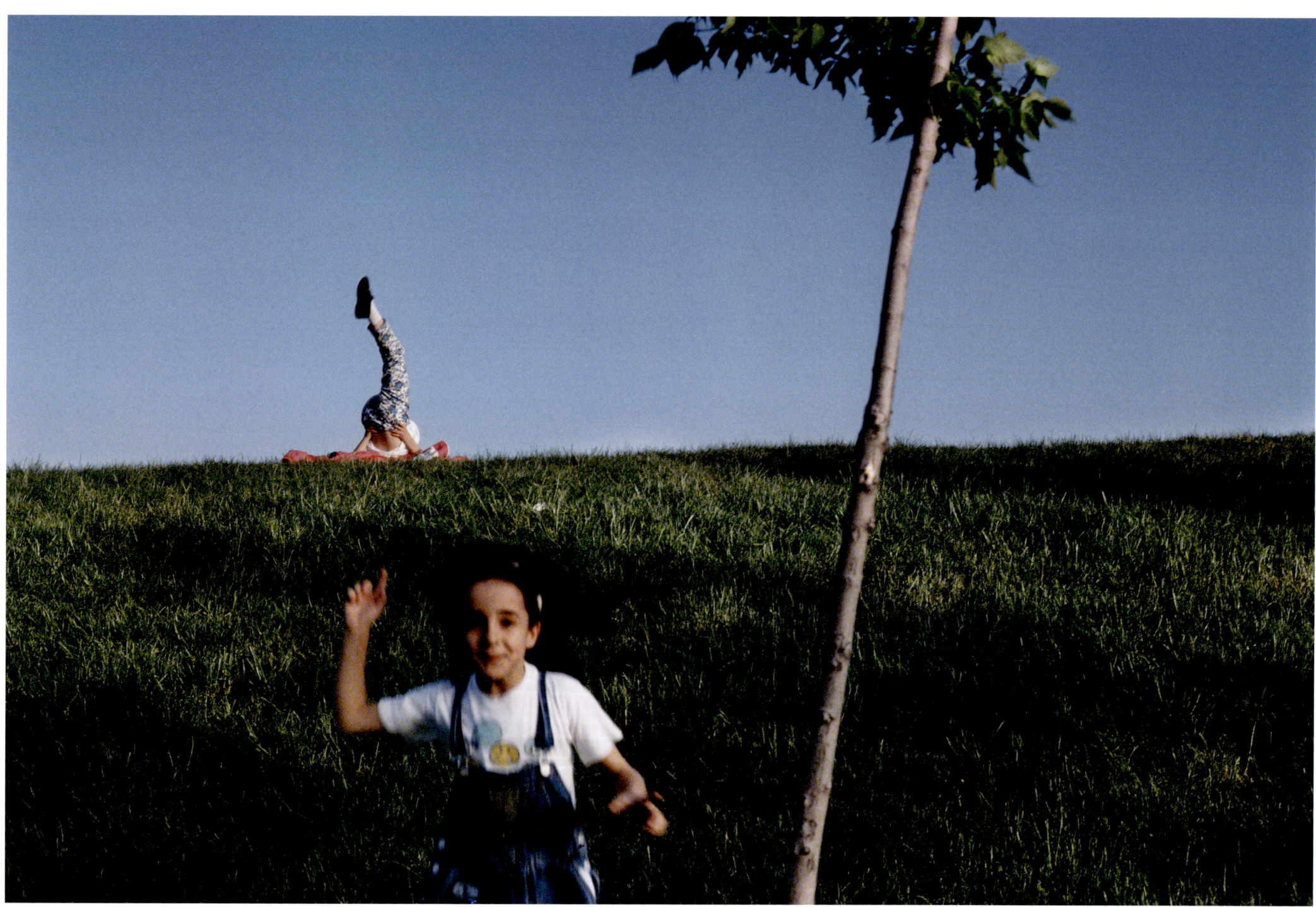

Madrid, 1992

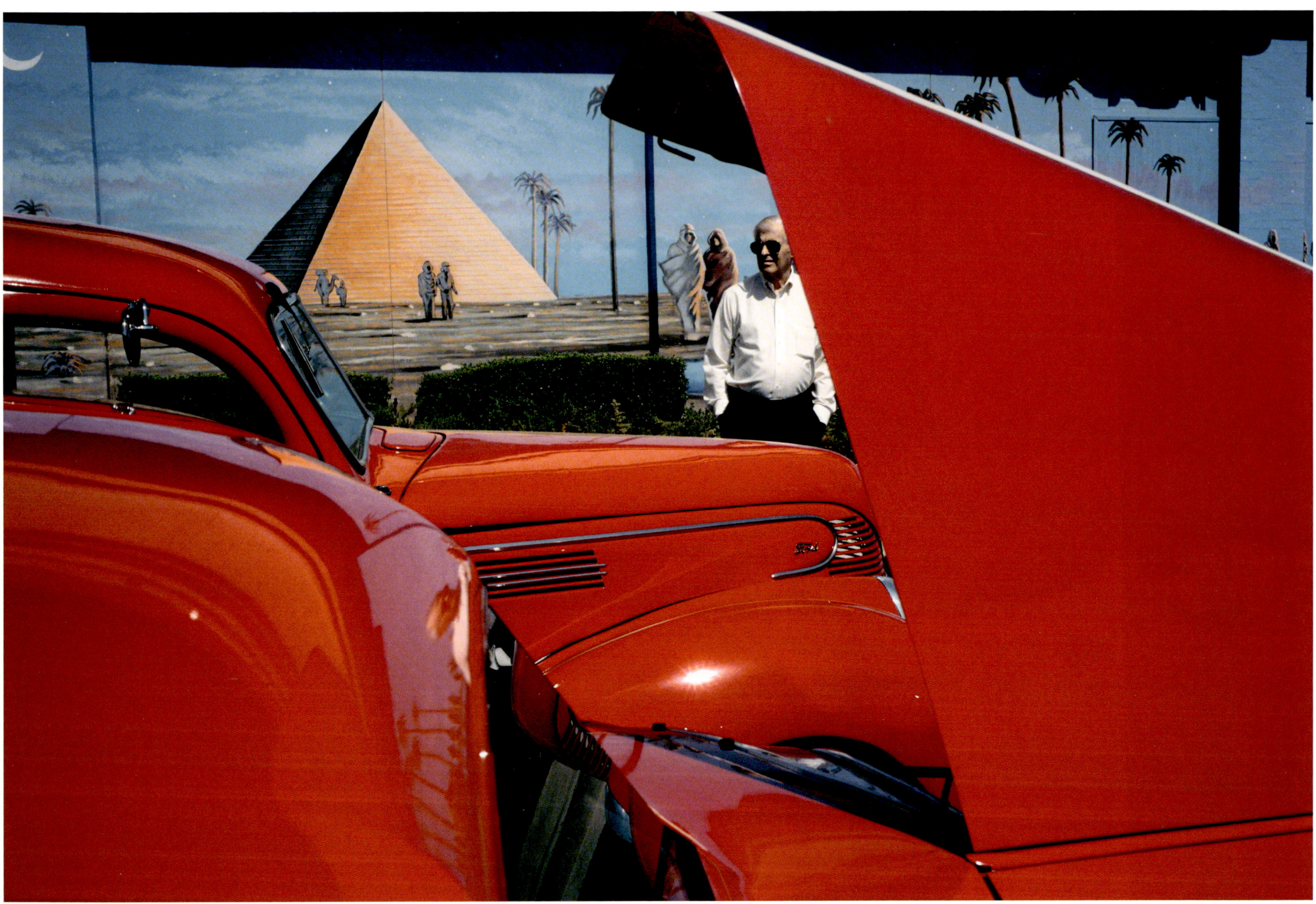

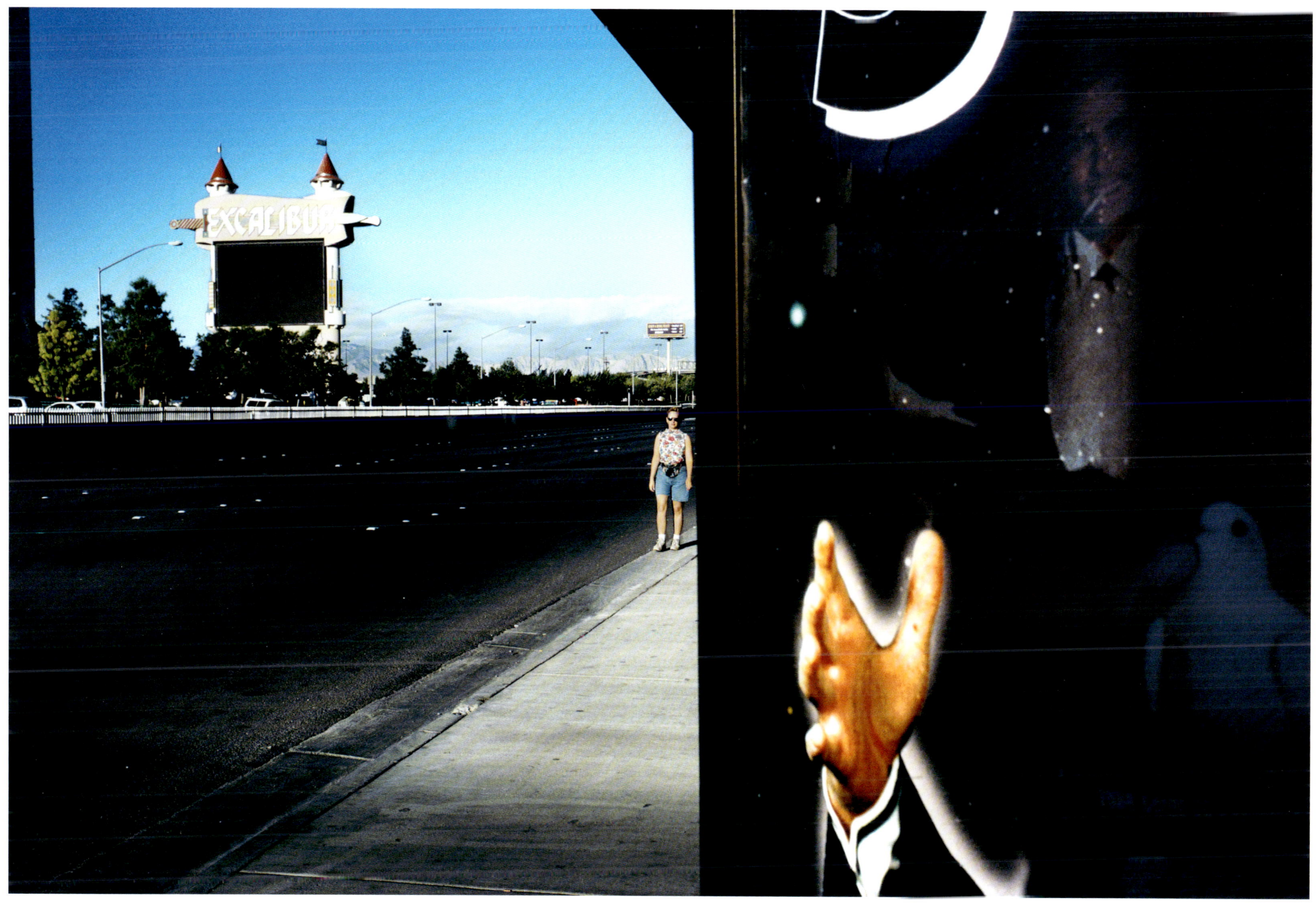

Las Vegas, 1997

Barcelona, 1992

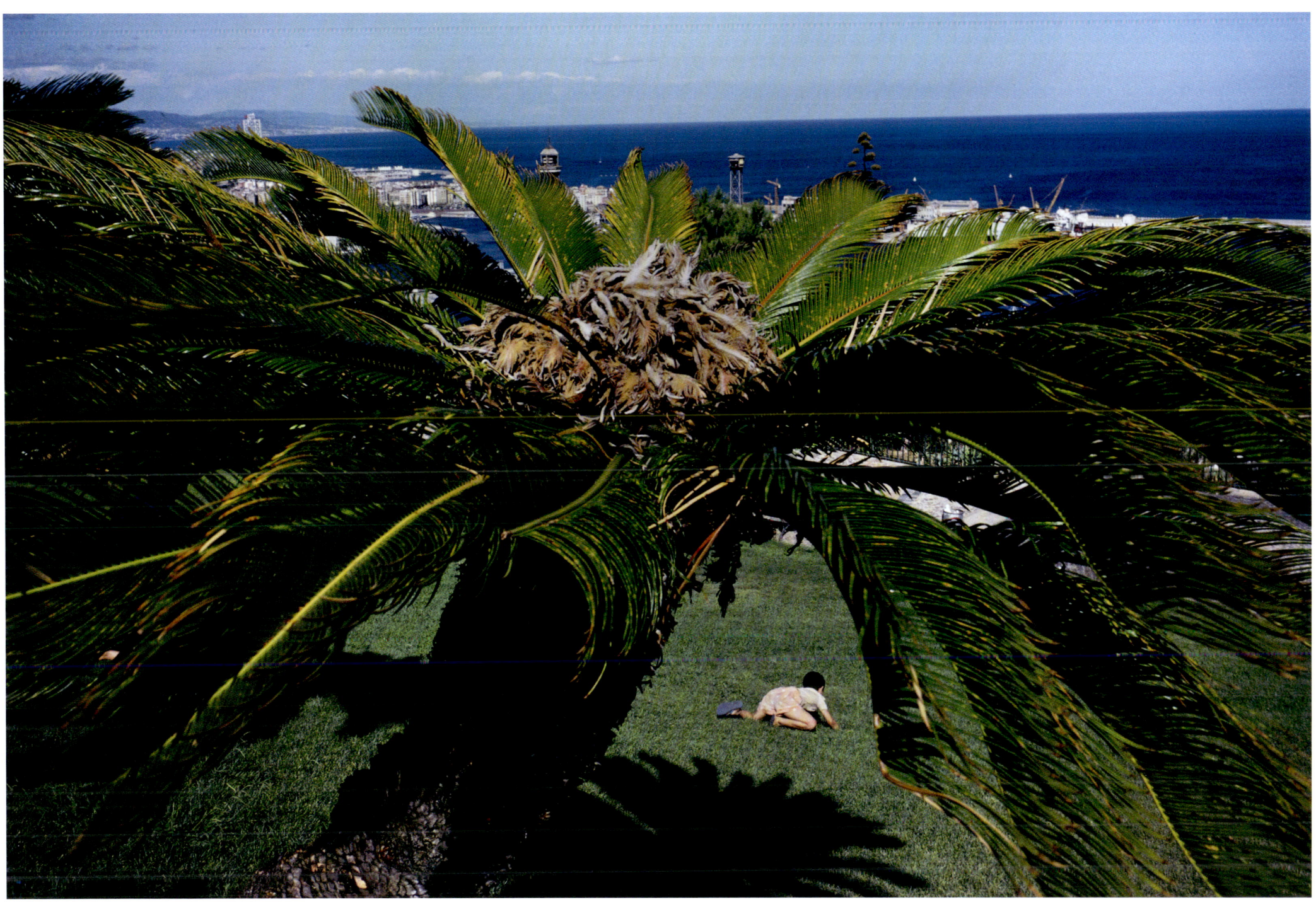

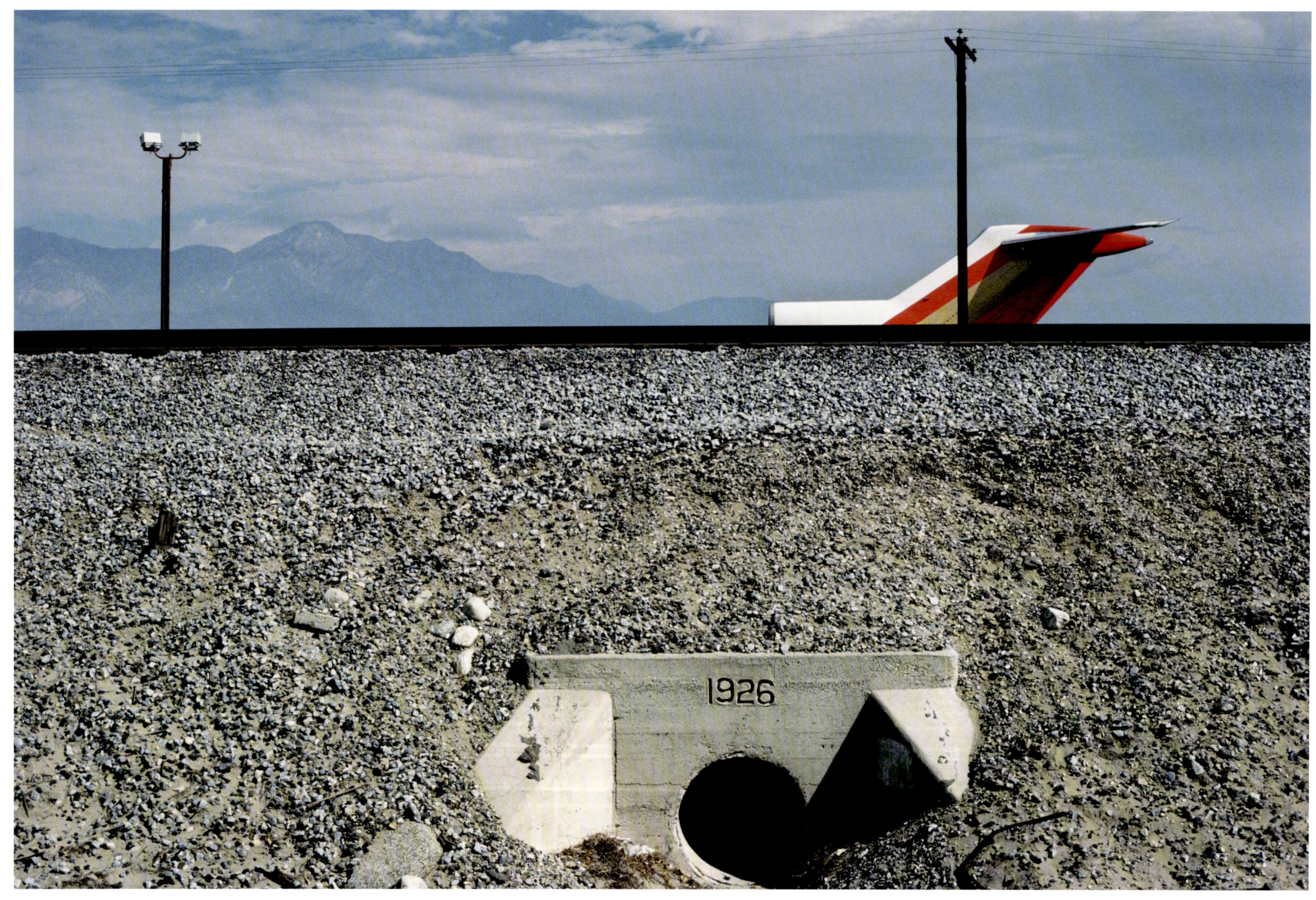

Ontario, California, 1998

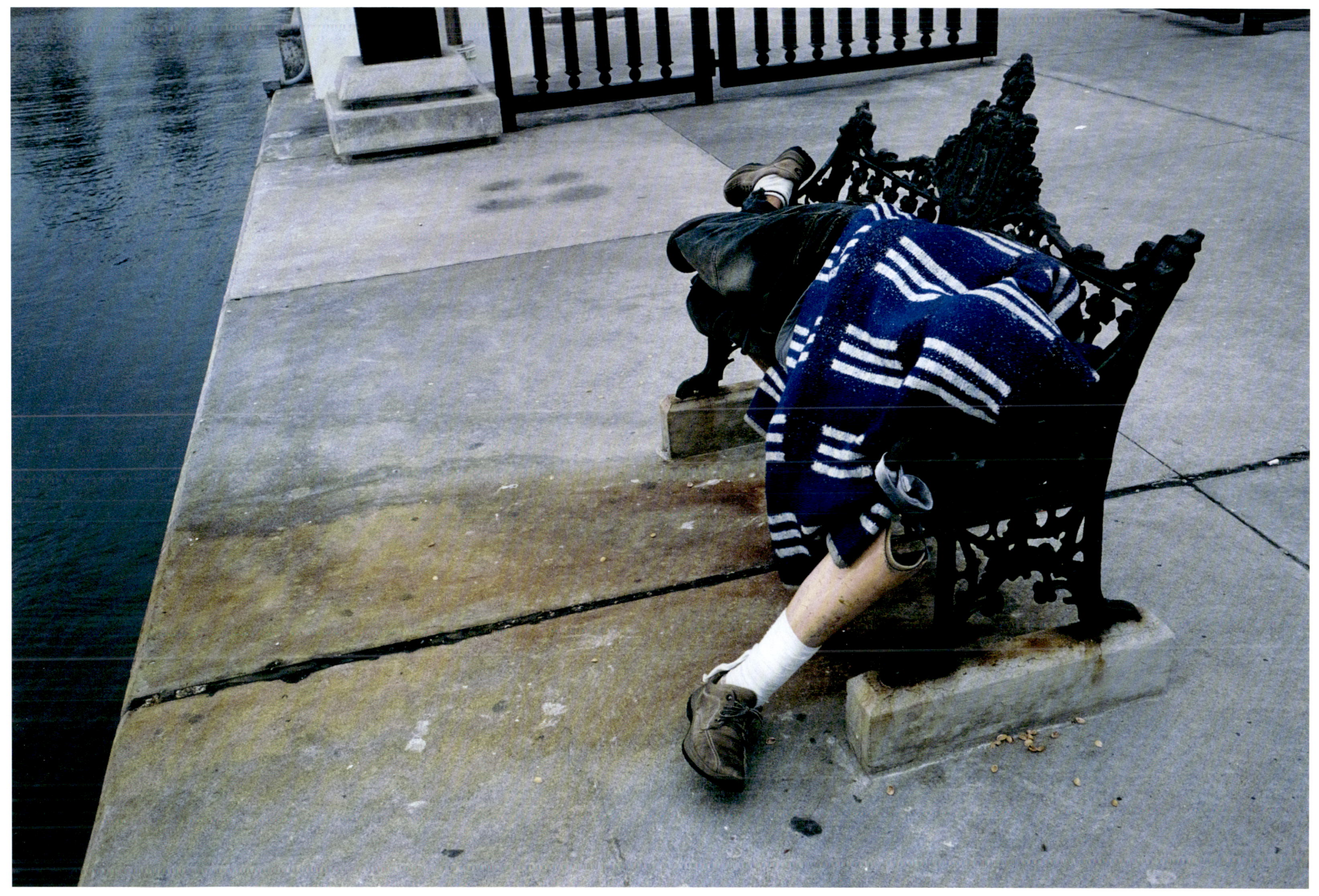

Veracruz, Mexico, 2003

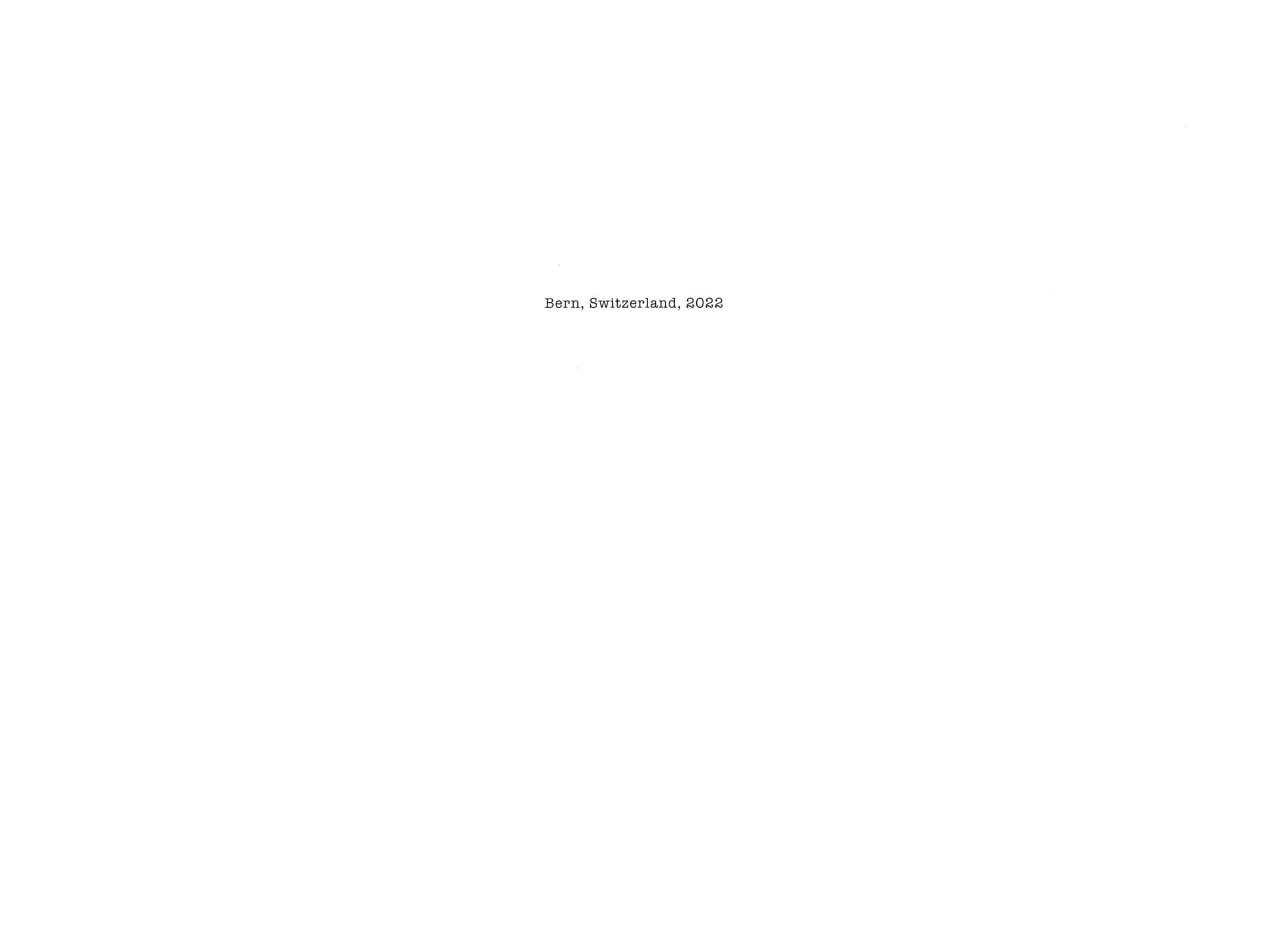

Bern, Switzerland, 2022

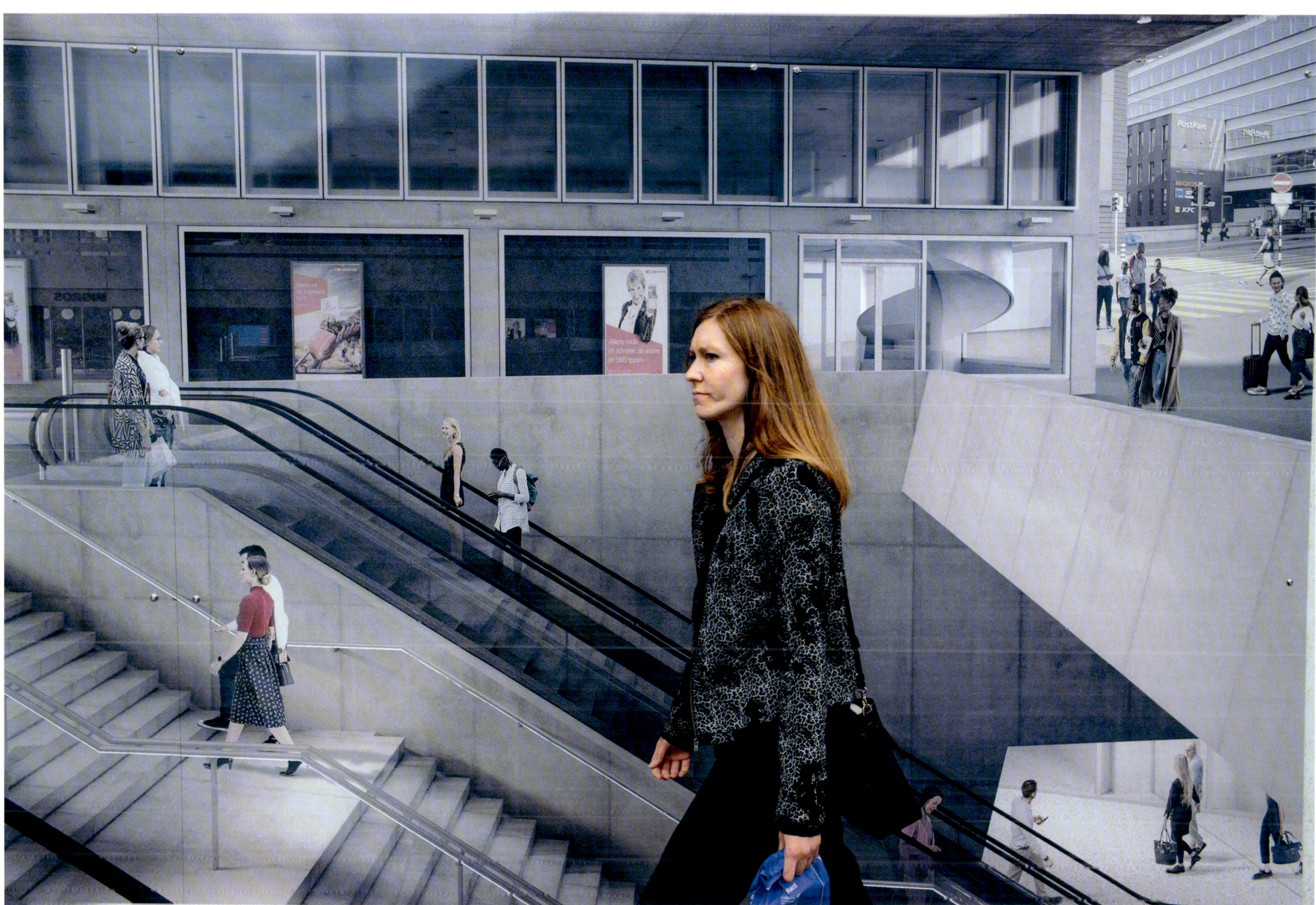

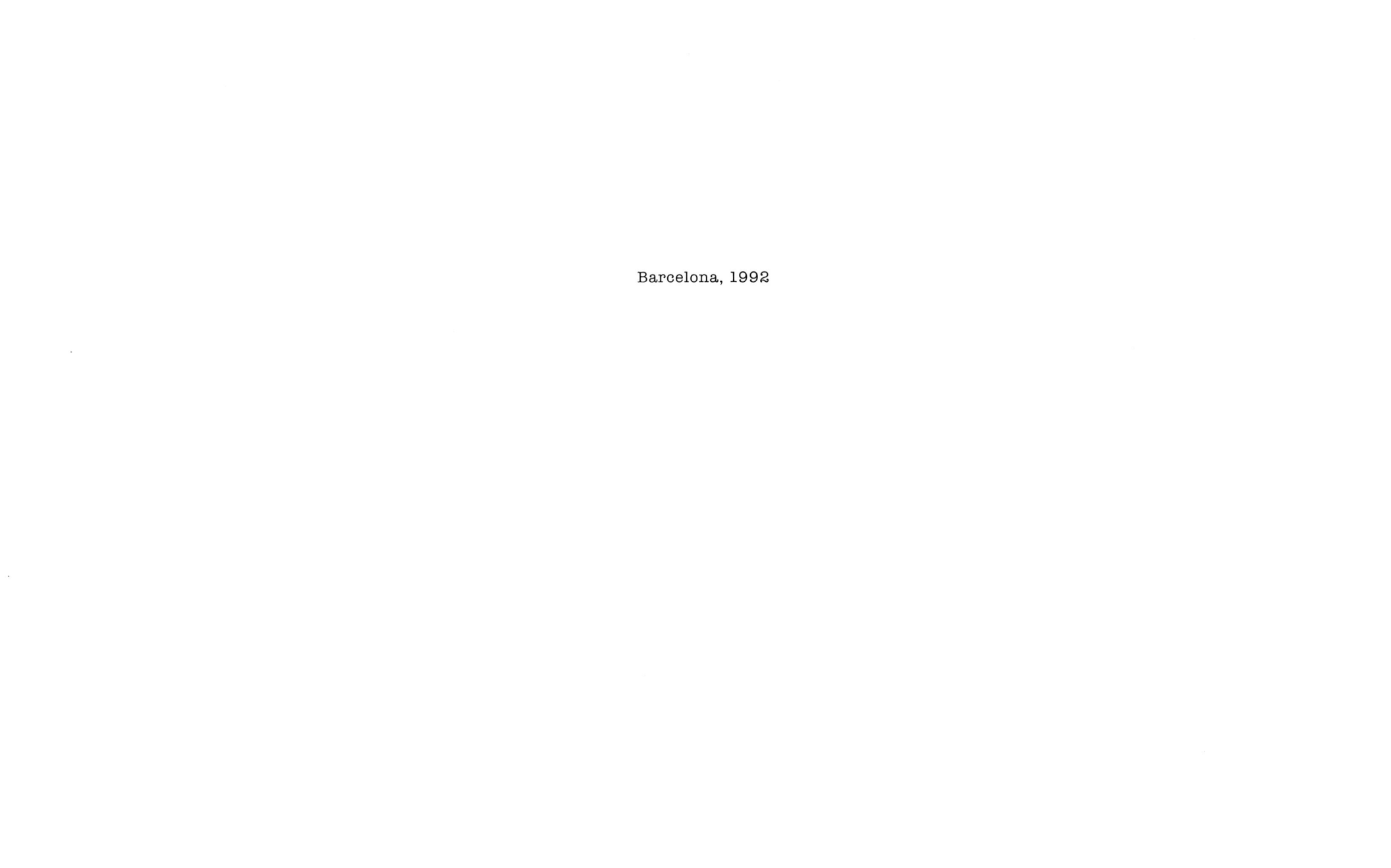

Barcelona, 1992

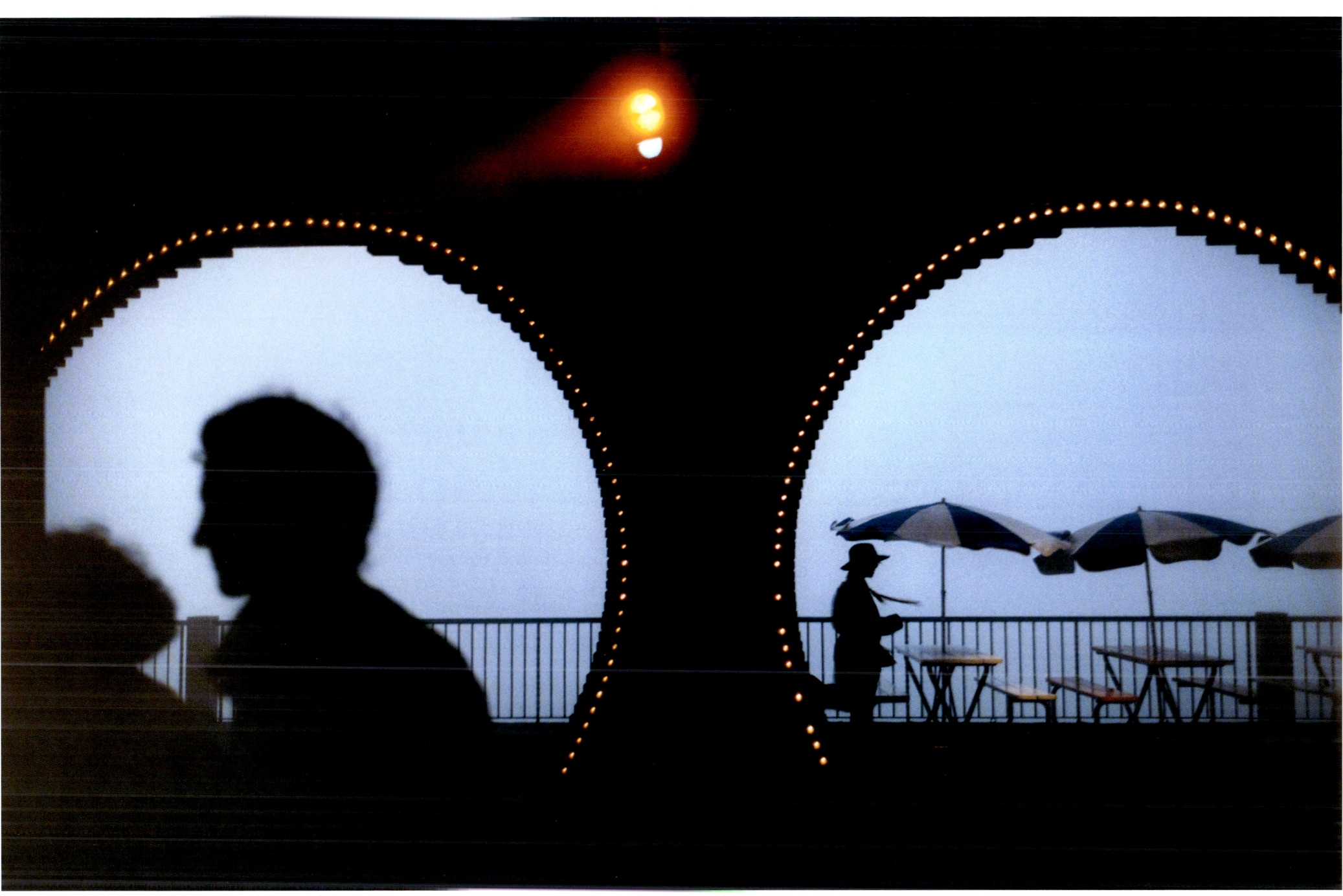

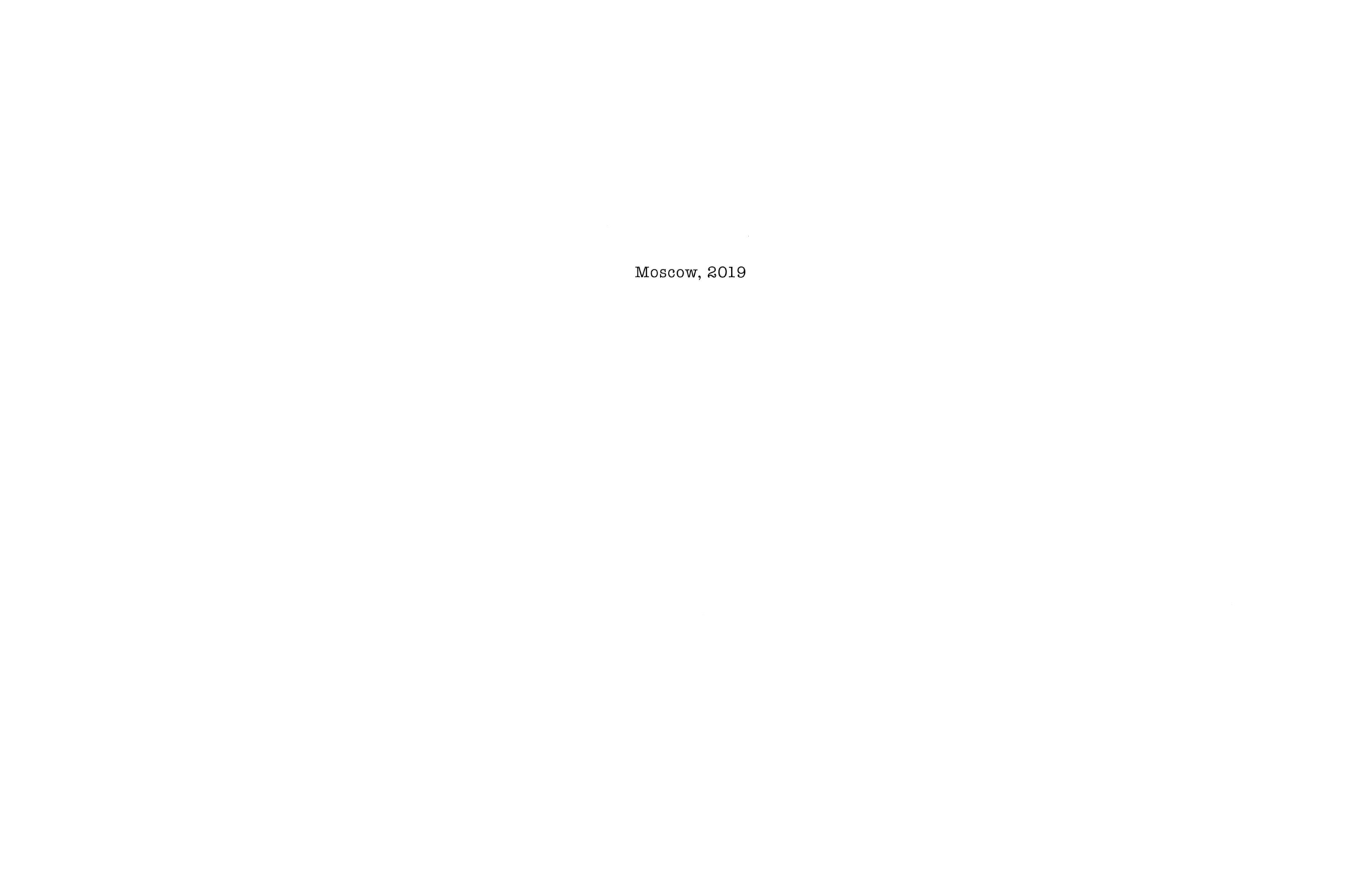

Moscow, 2019

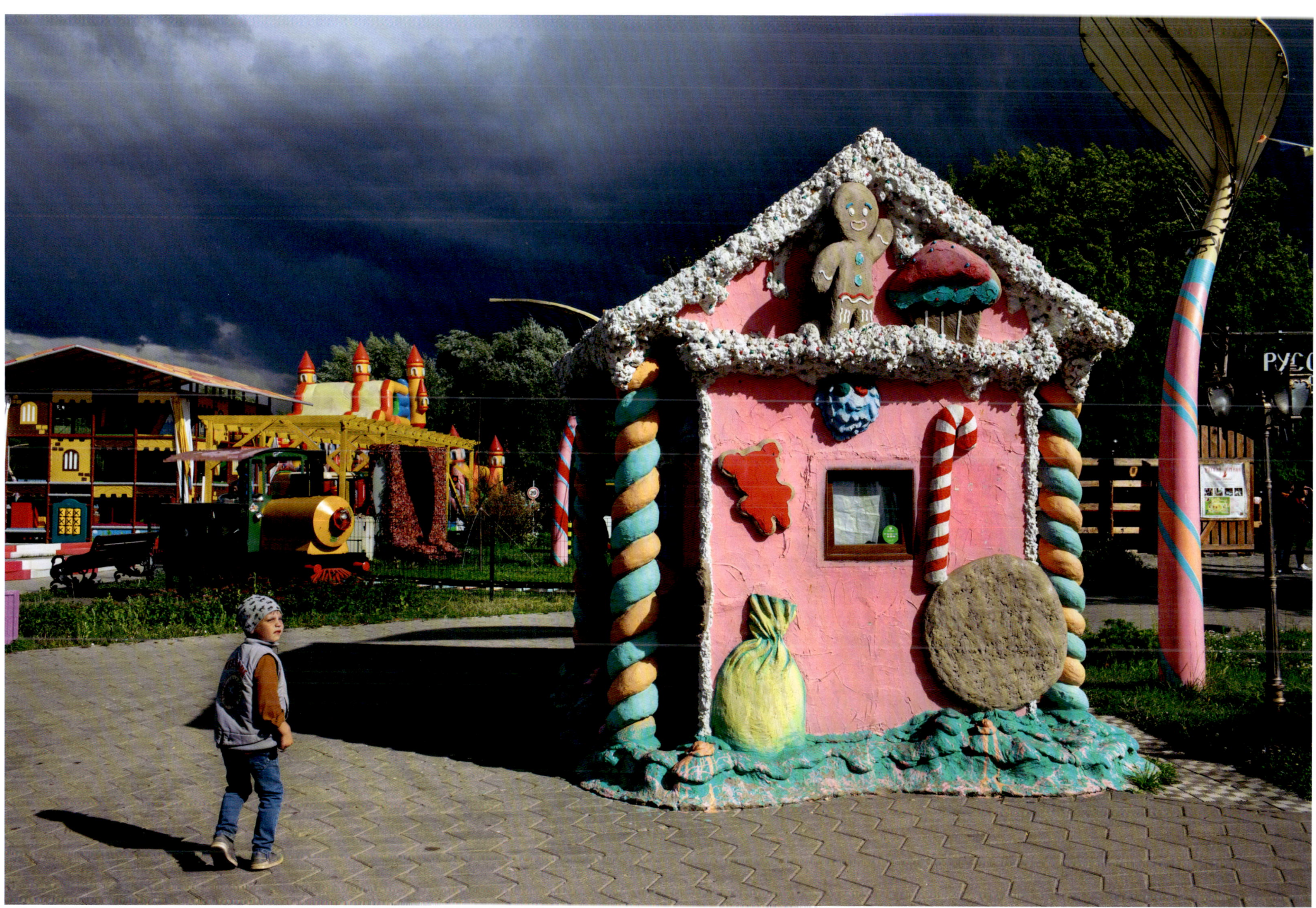

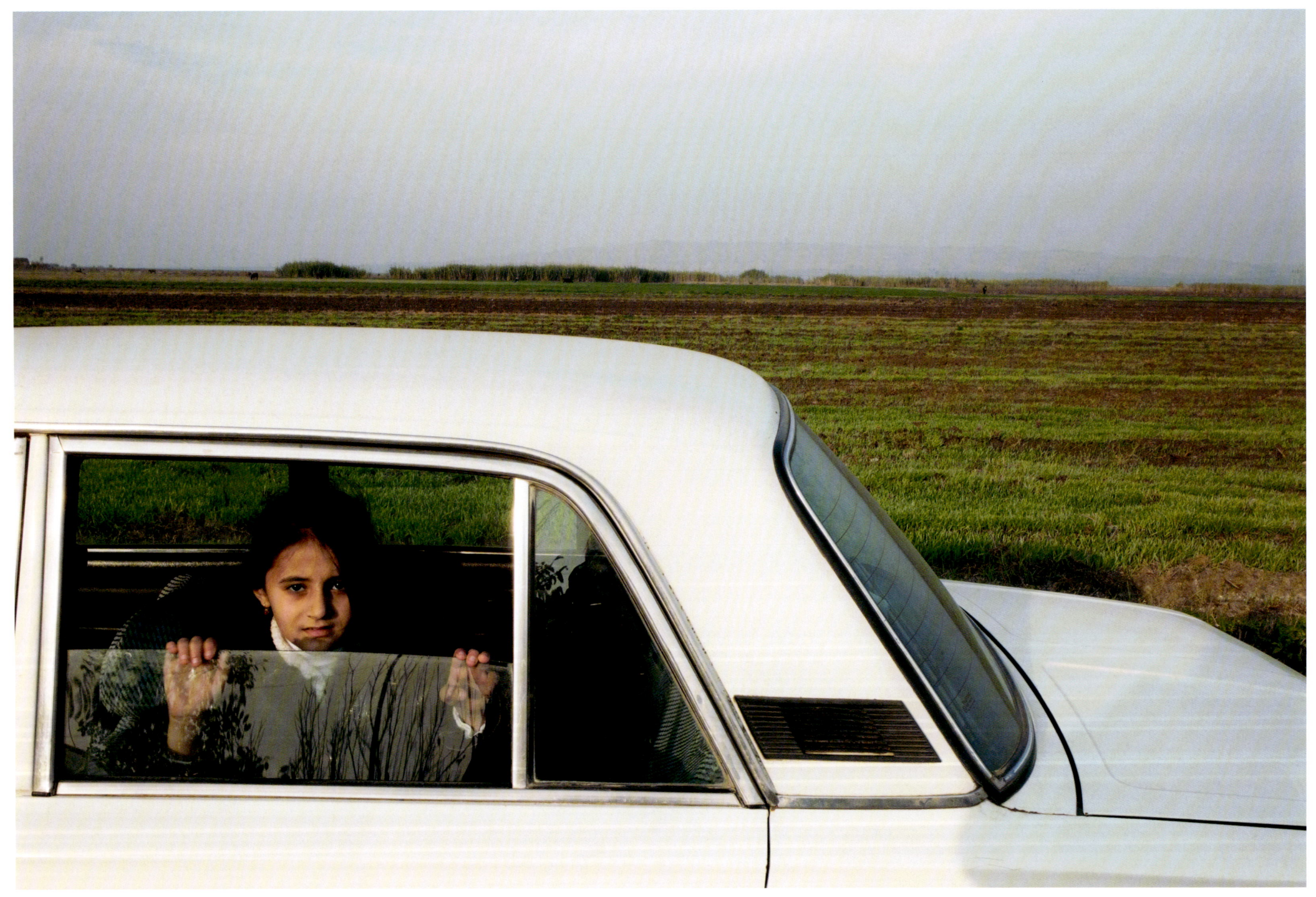

Eyvazlilar, Azerbaijan, 2009

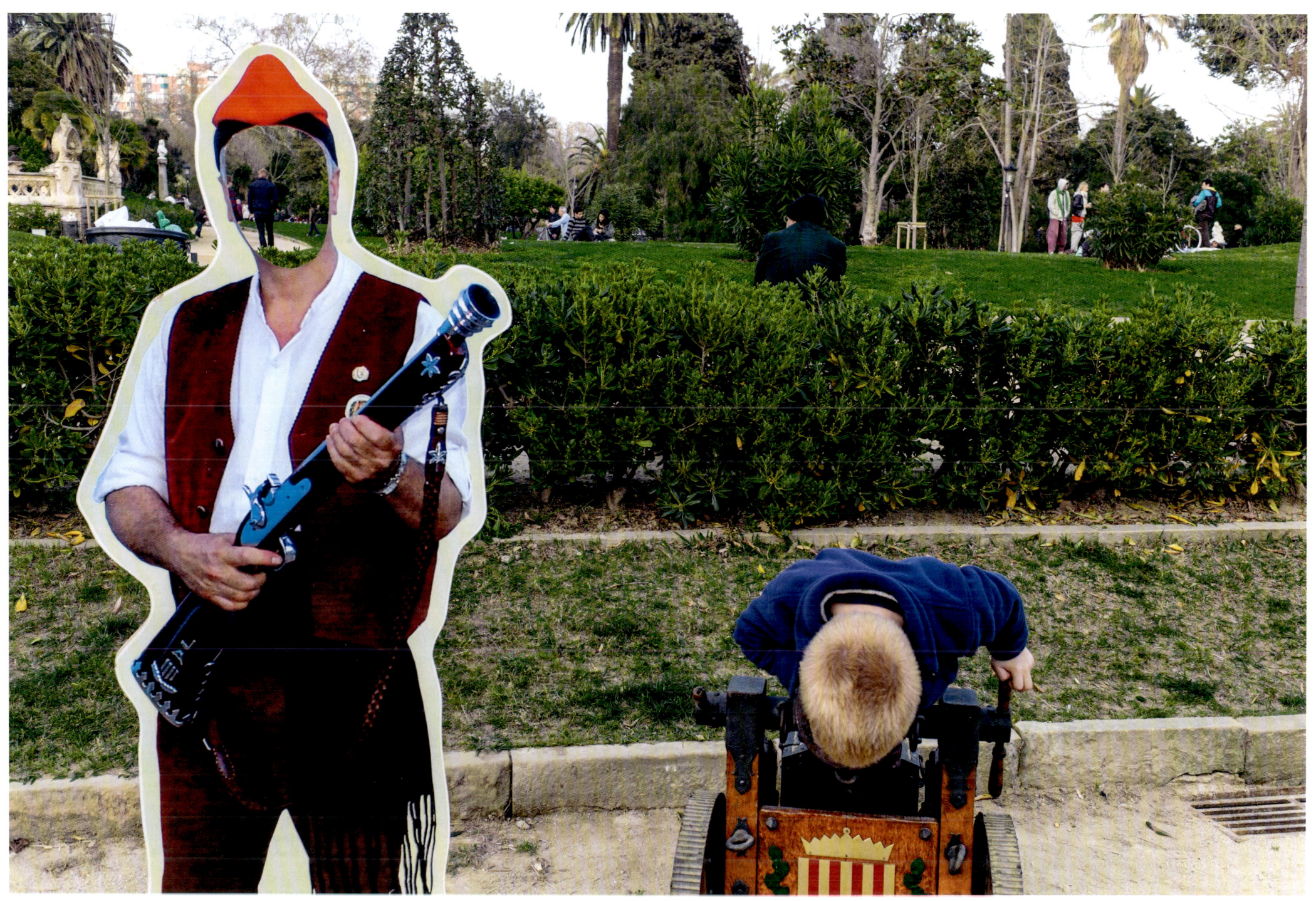

Barcelona, 2011

Mountain, North Dakota, 2019

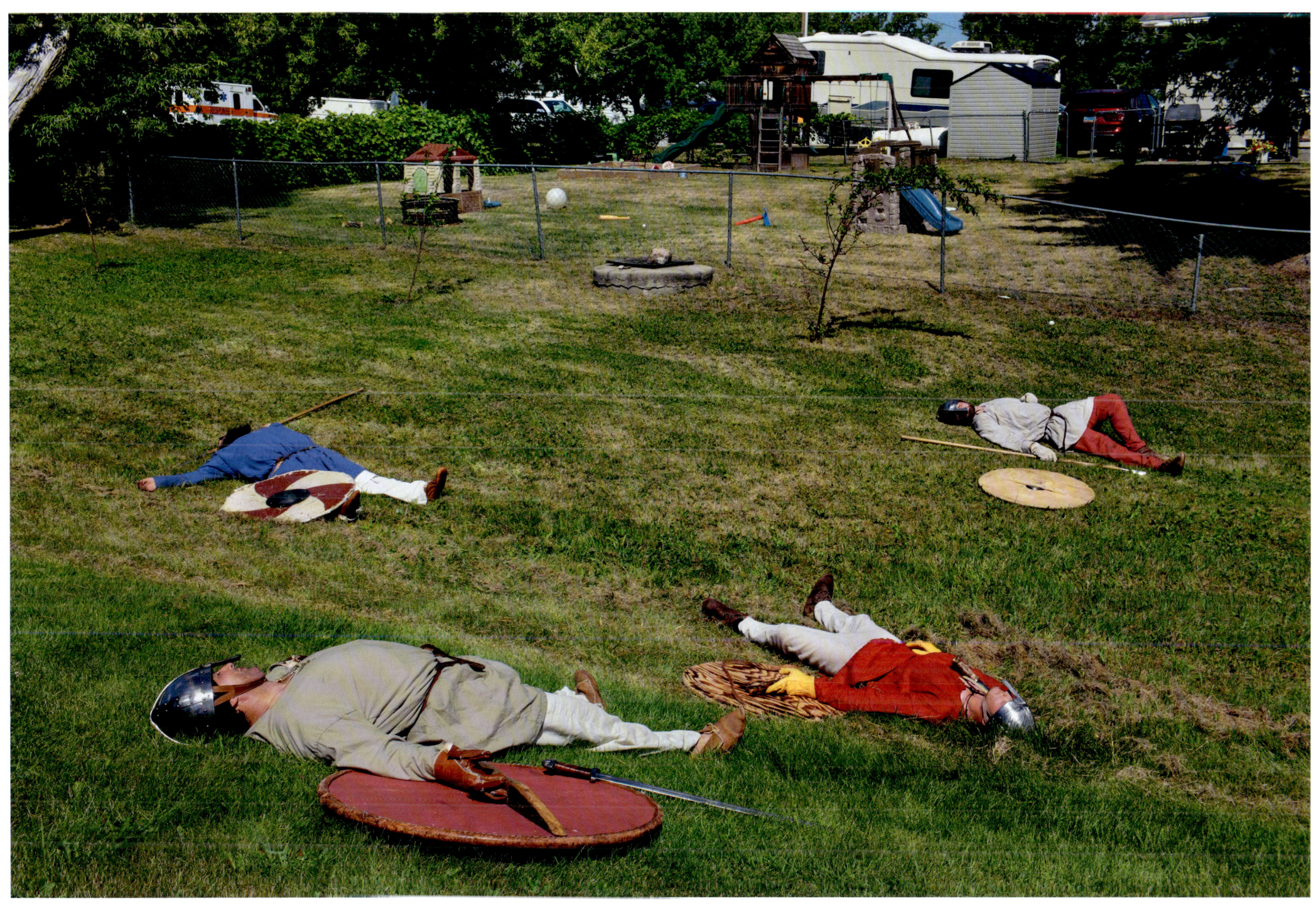

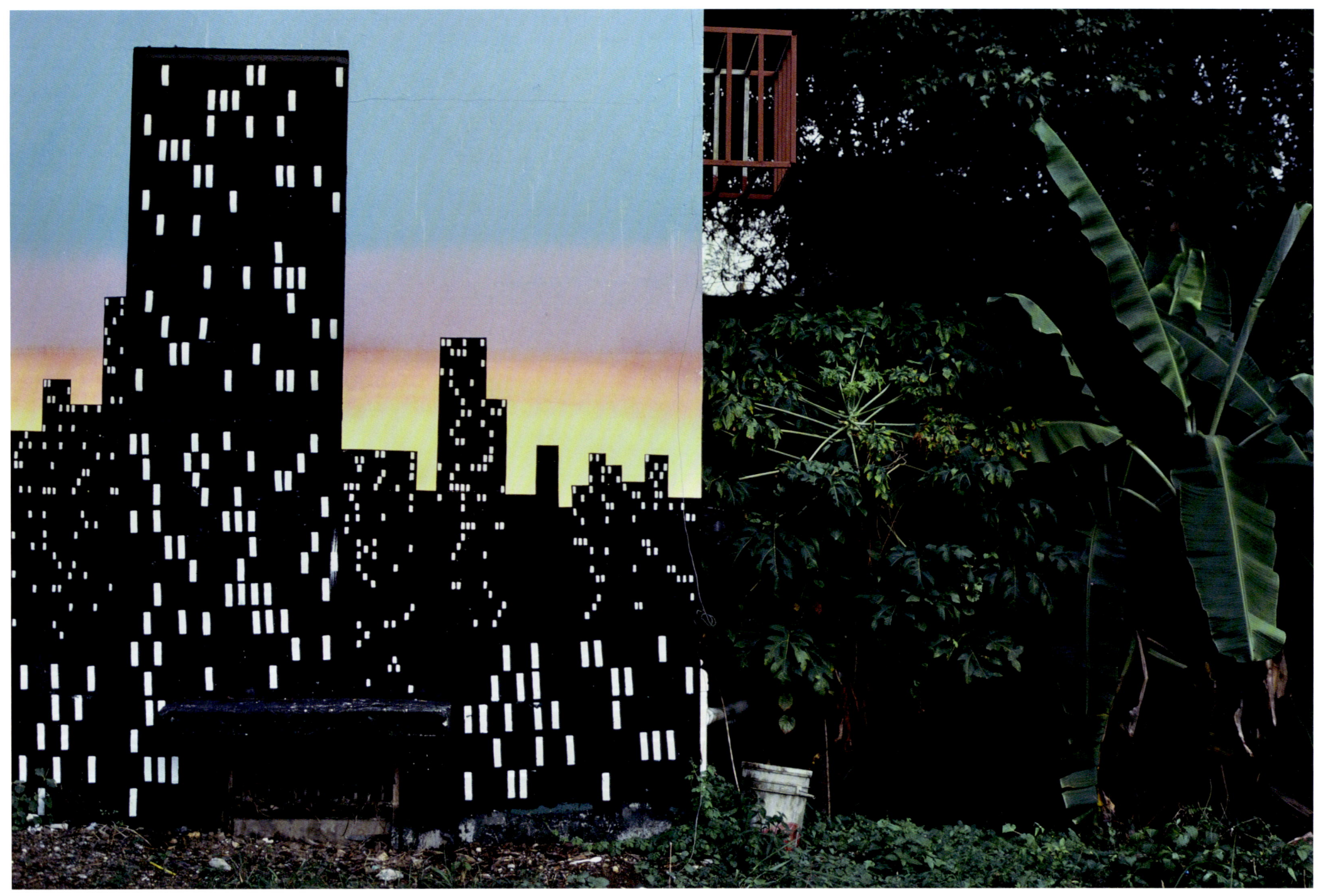

Near Coamo, Puerto Rico, 1990

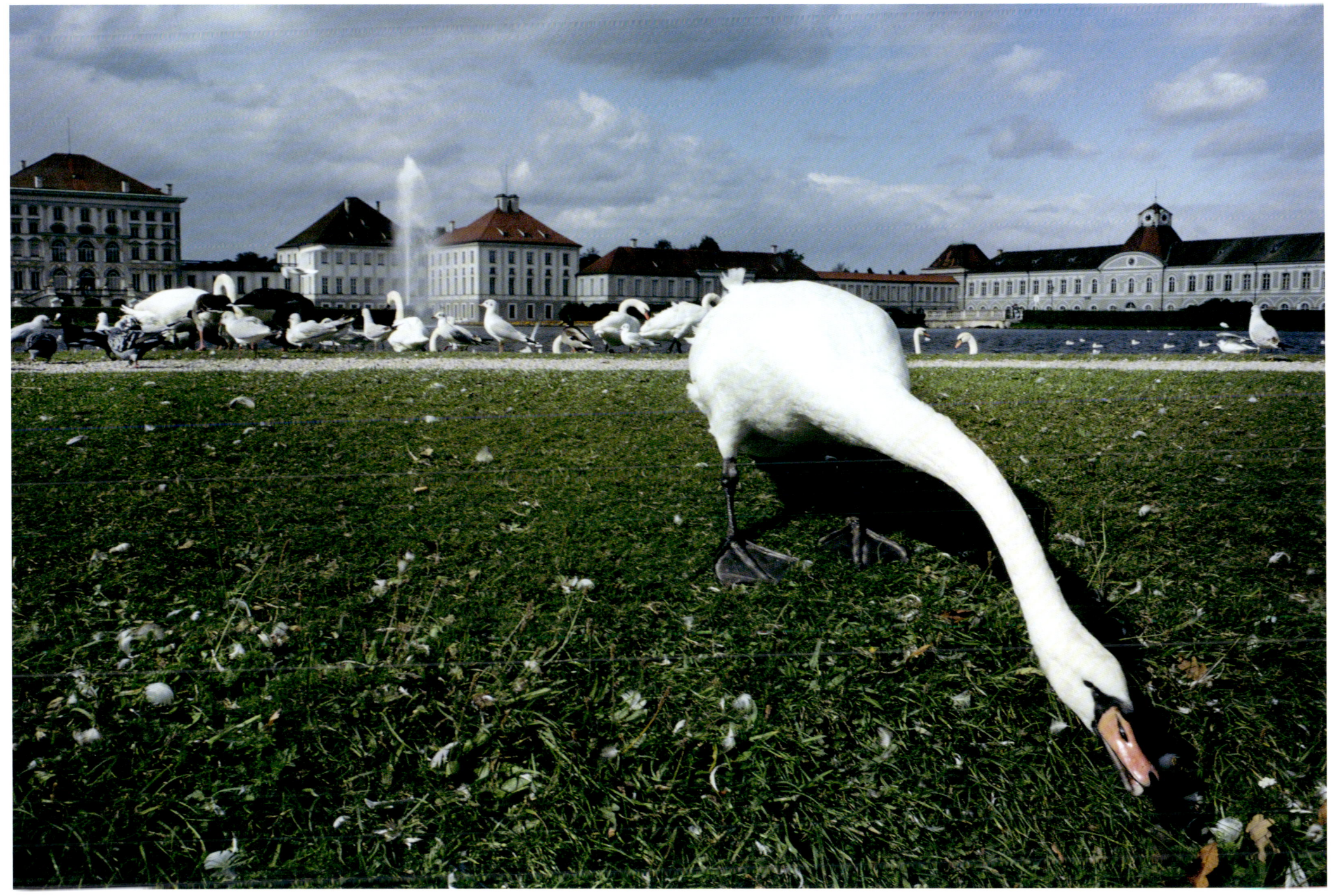

Munich, 1991

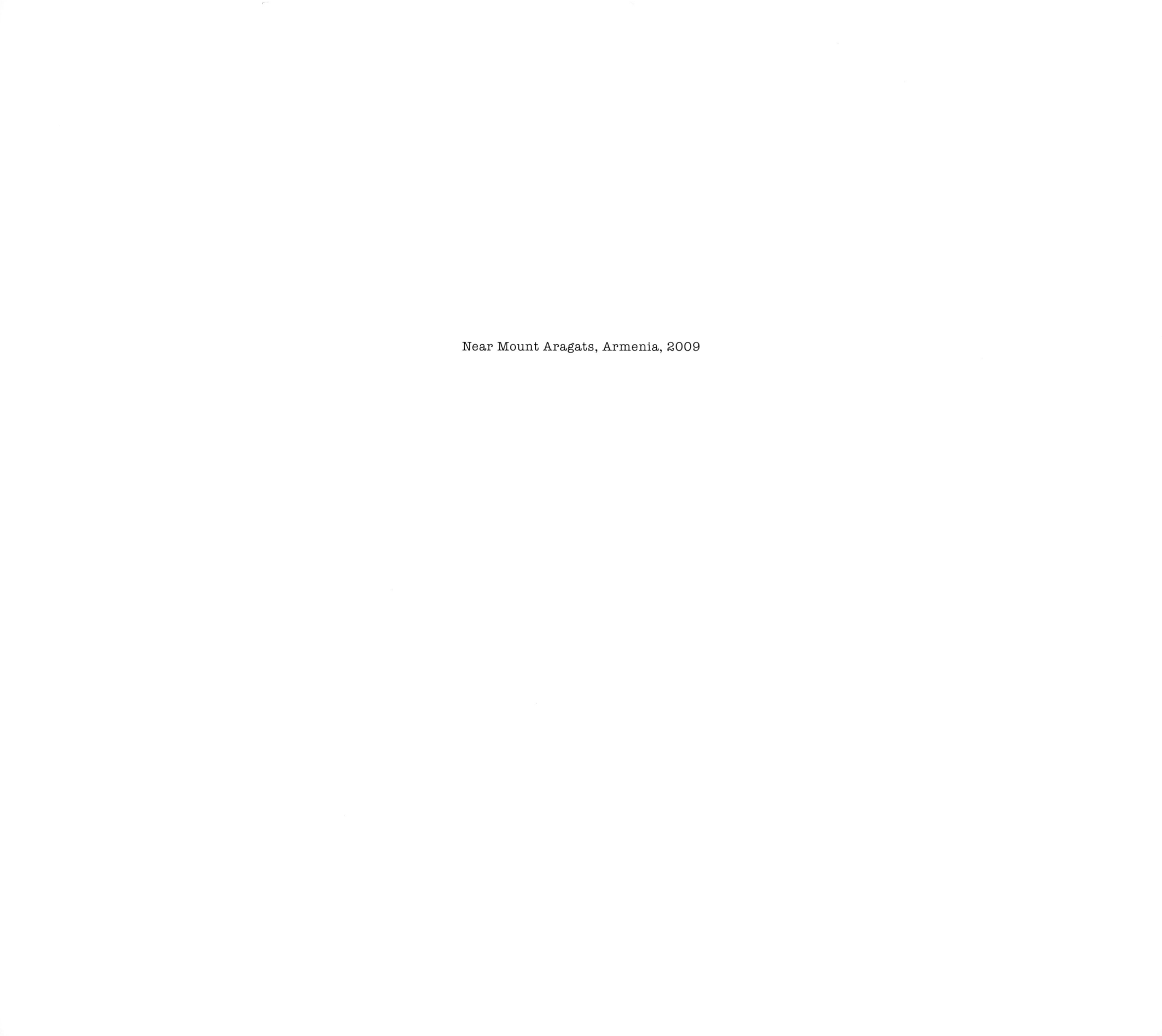

Near Mount Aragats, Armenia, 2009

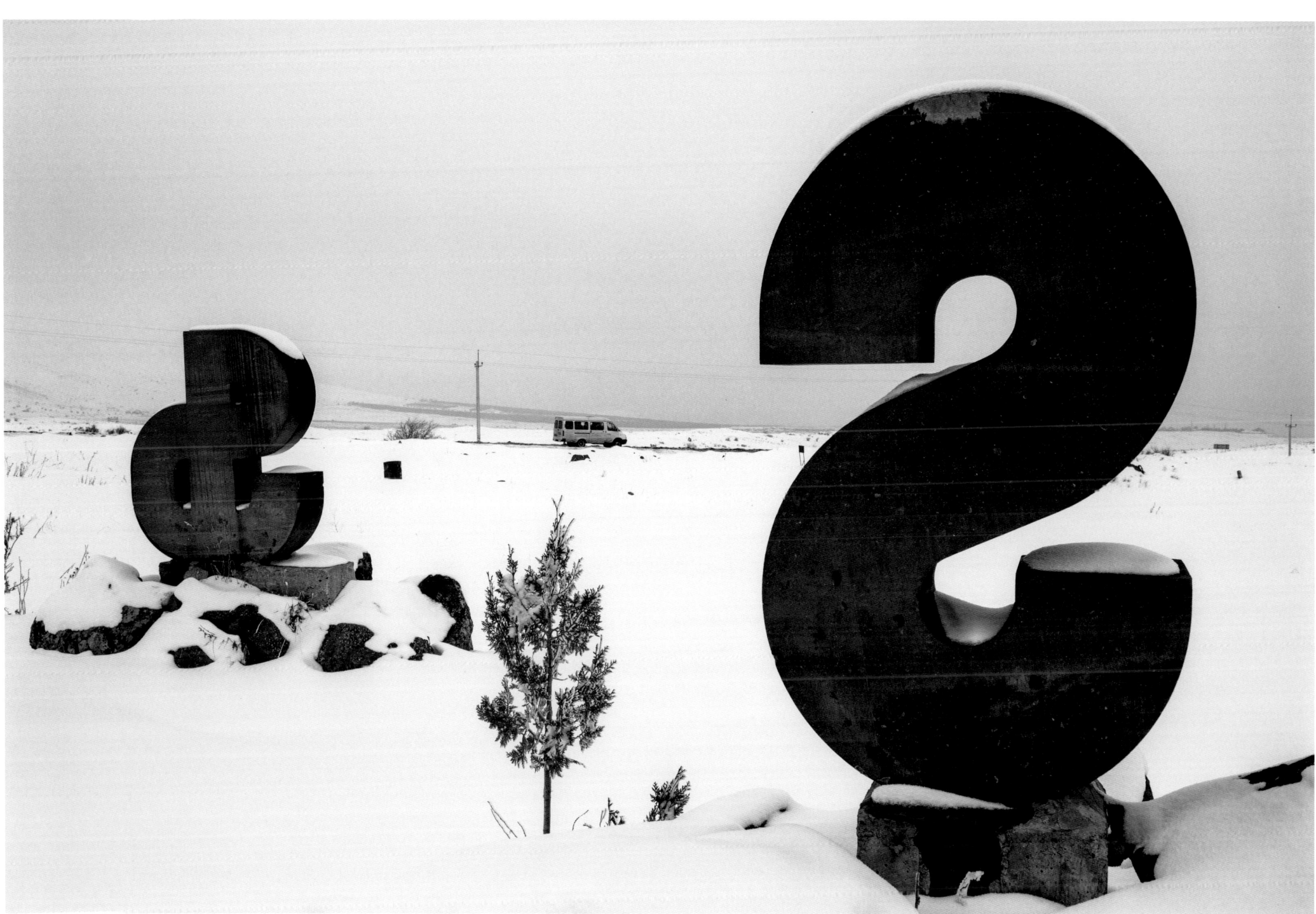

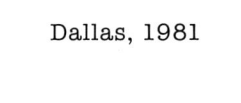

Dallas, 1981

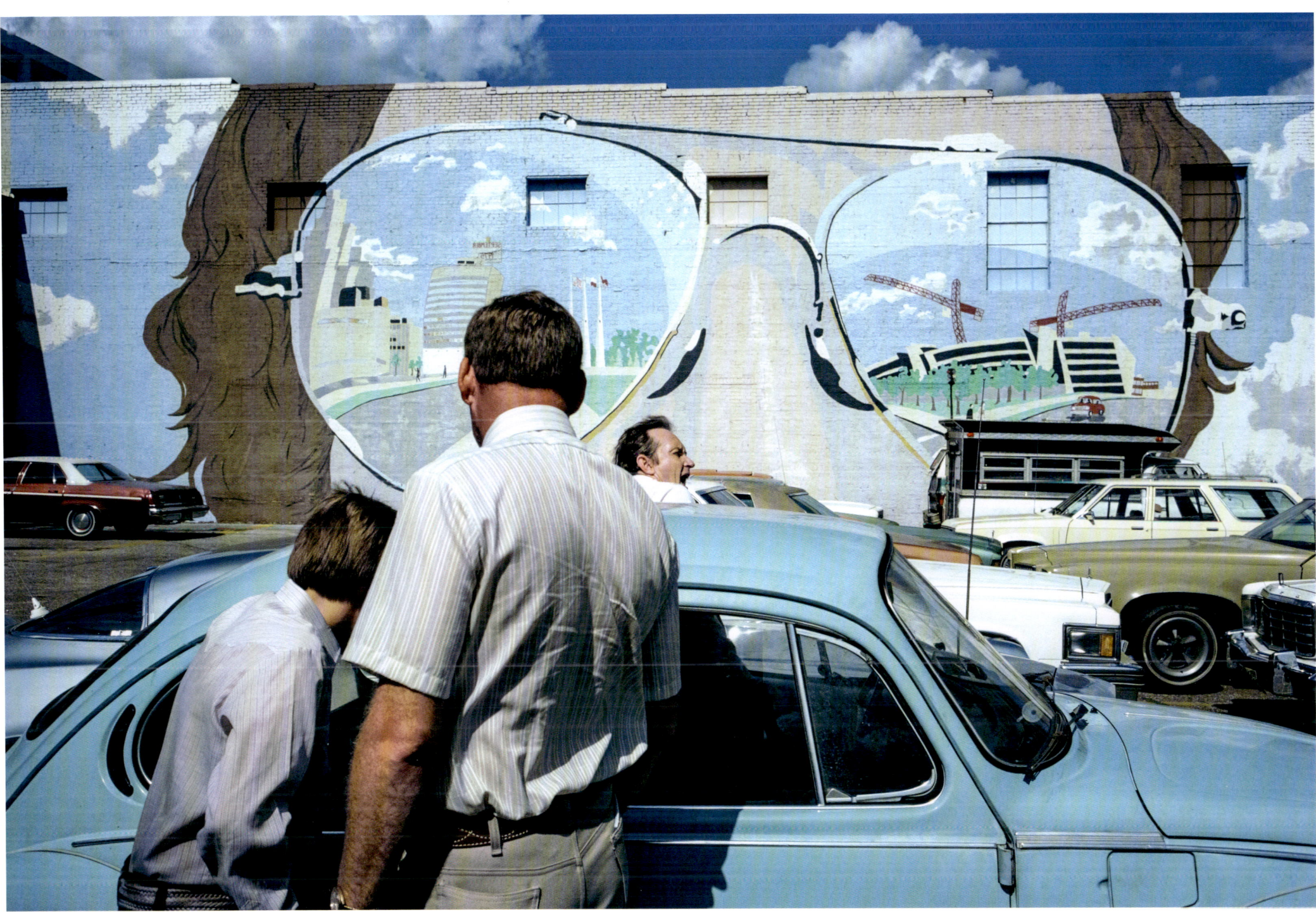

Piñones, Puerto Rico, 1990

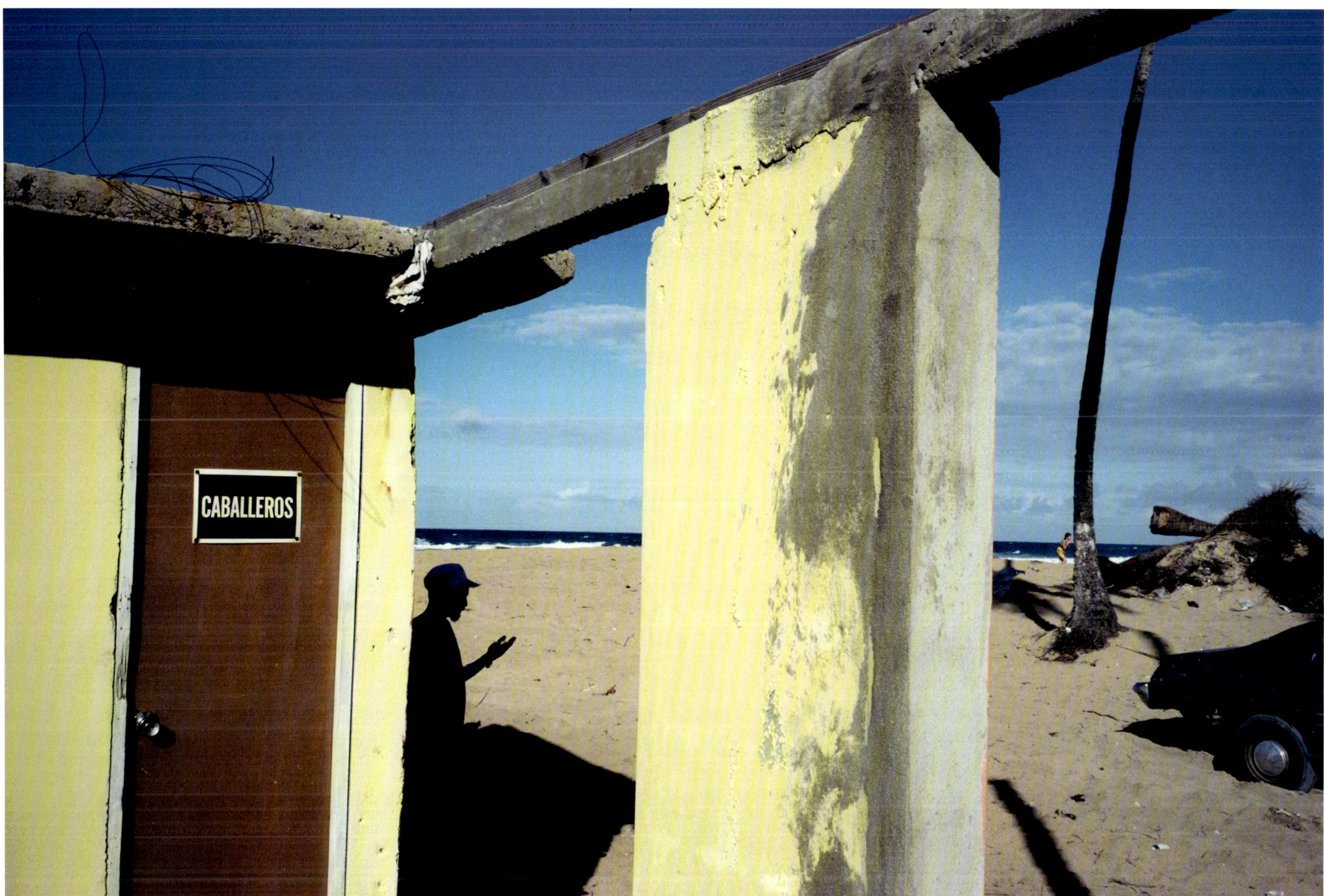

Durban, South Africa, 1994

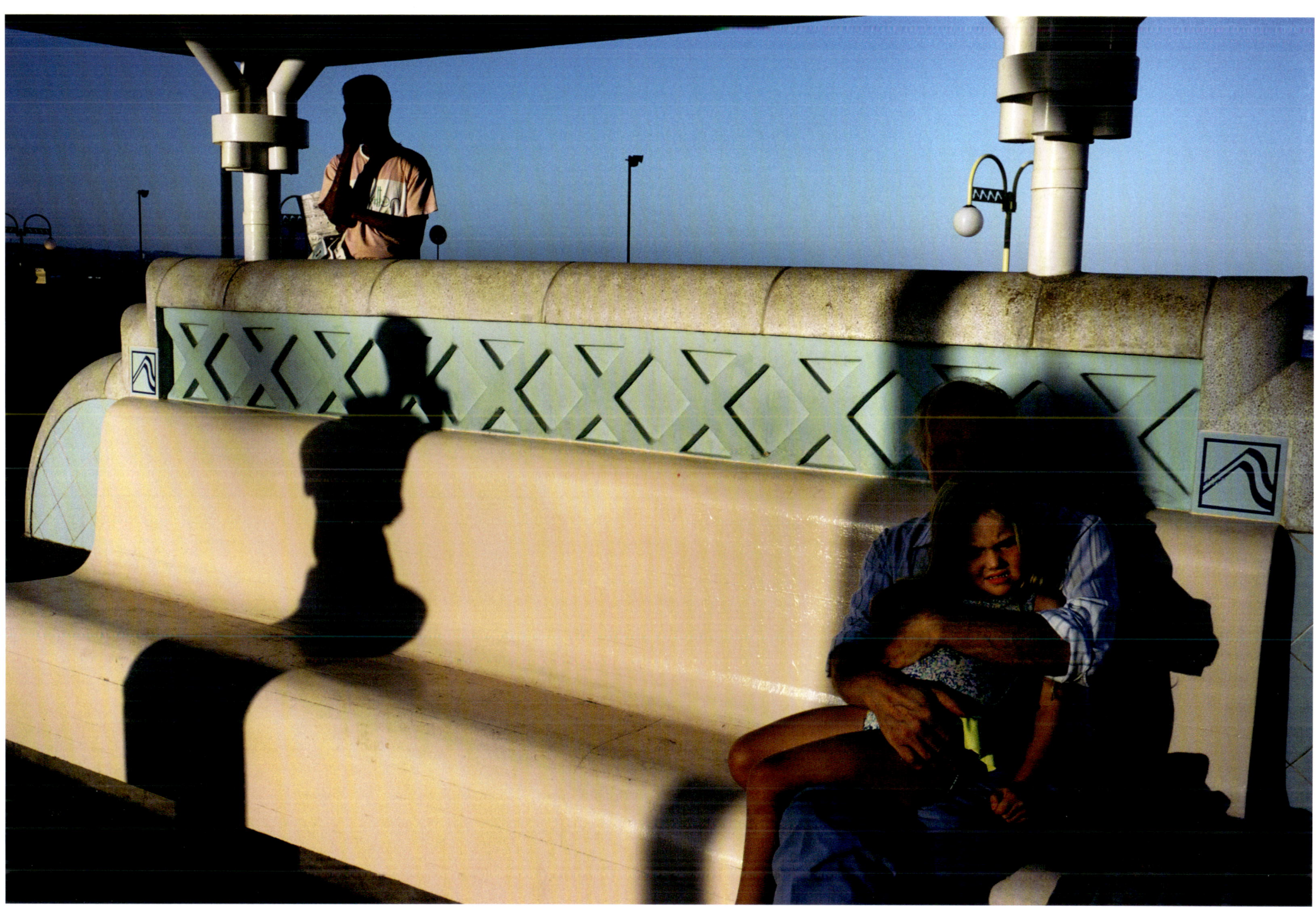

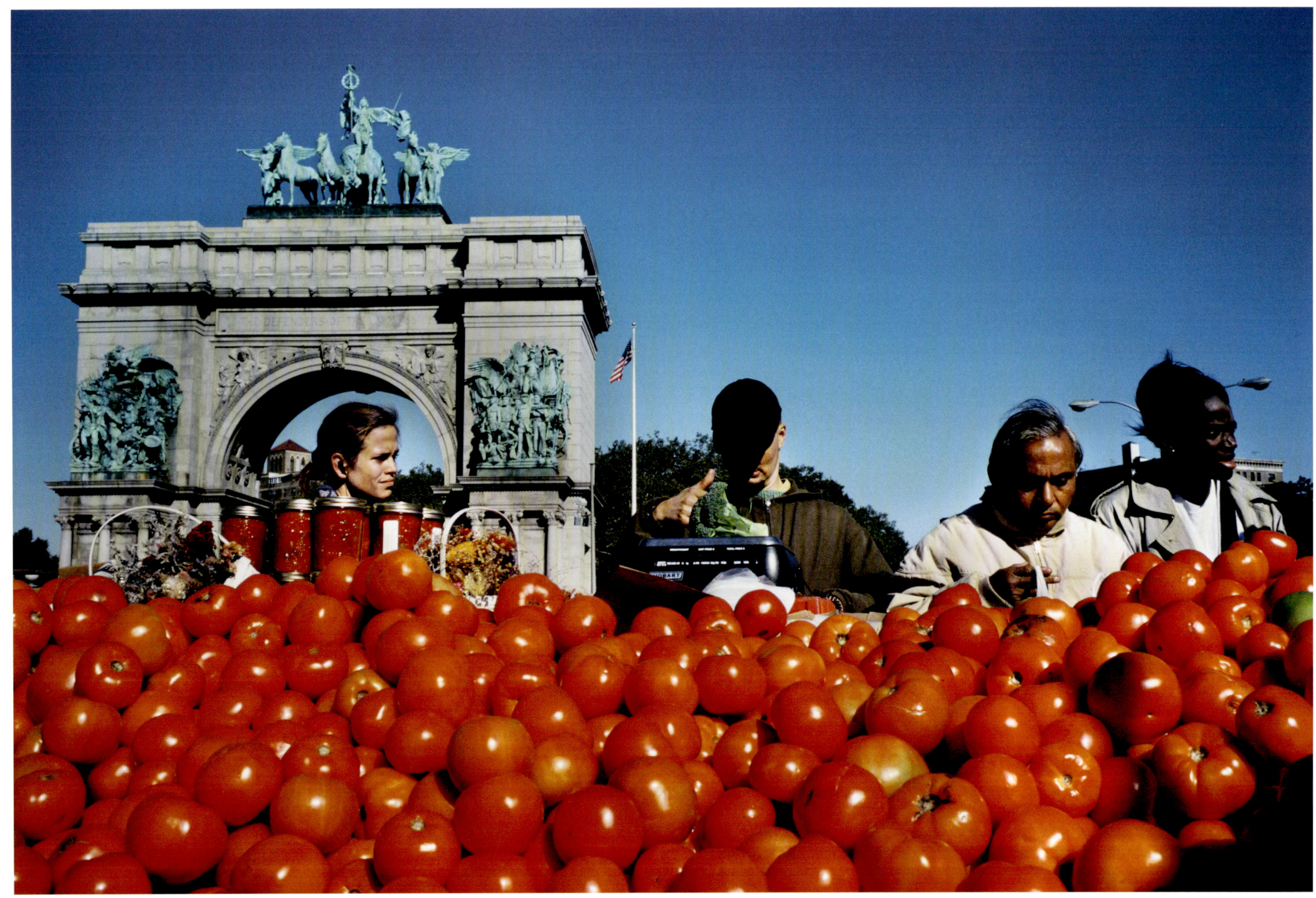

Brooklyn, 1994

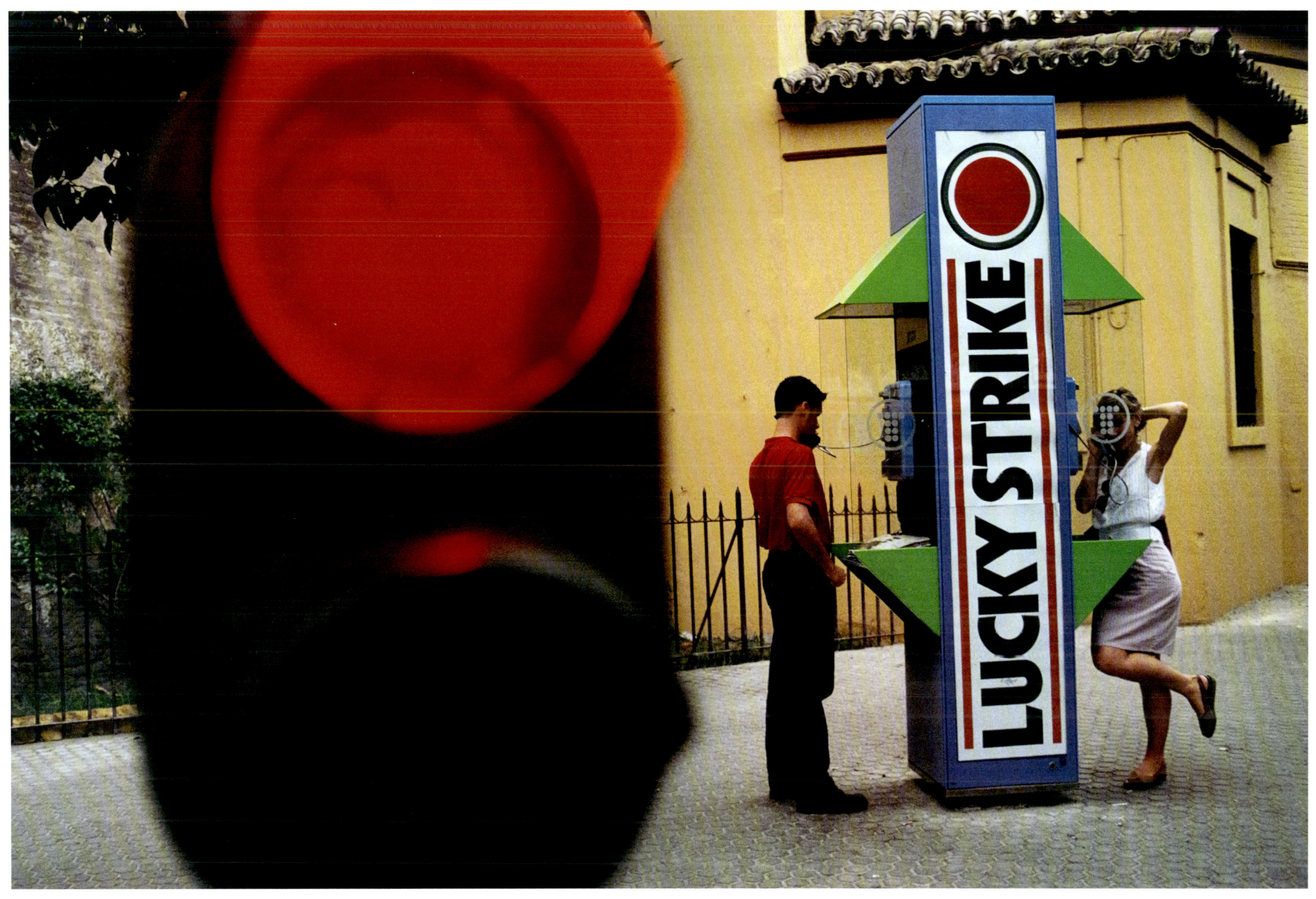

Barcelona, 1992

Bern, Switzerland, 2022

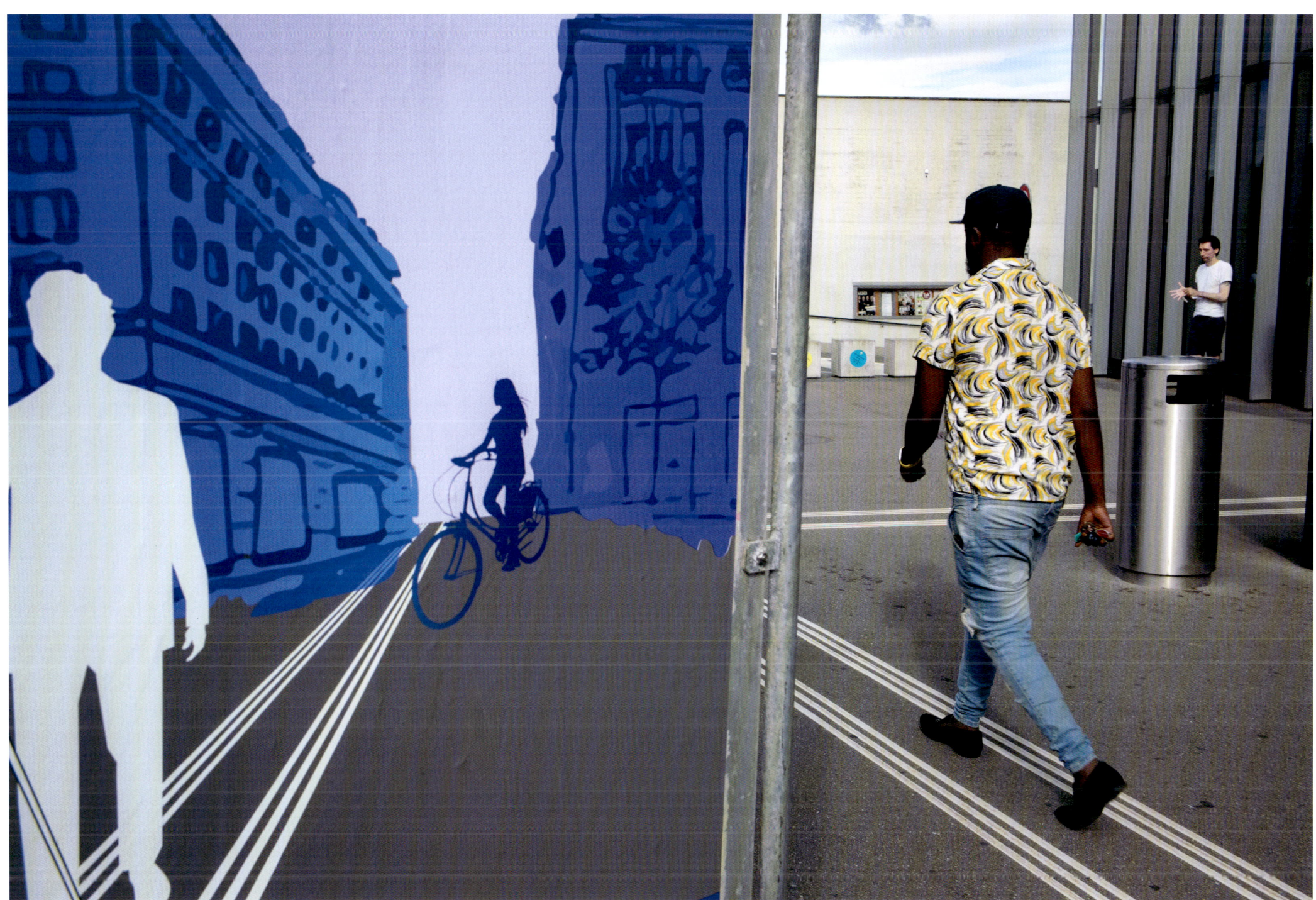

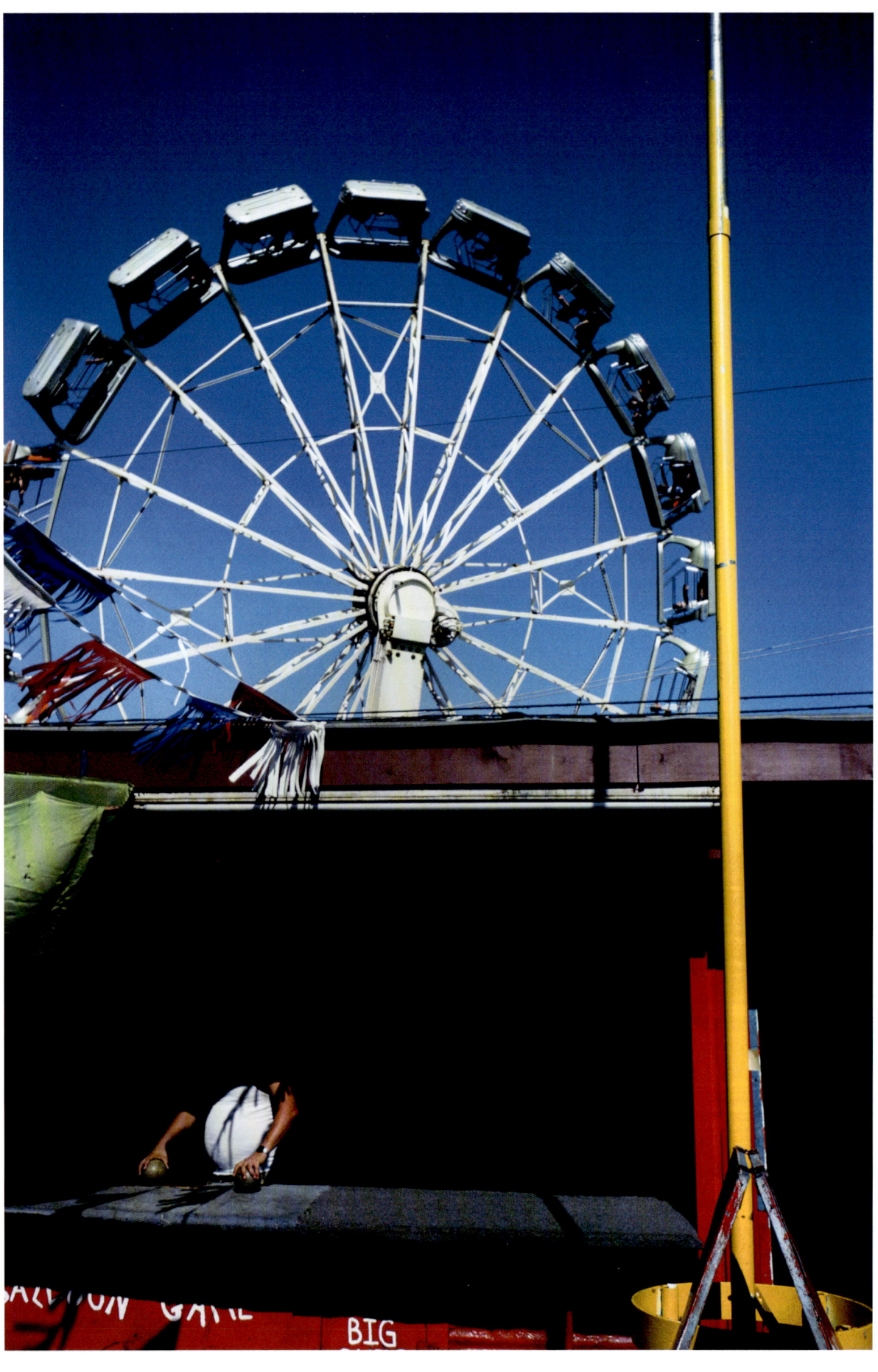

Coney Island, New York, 1983

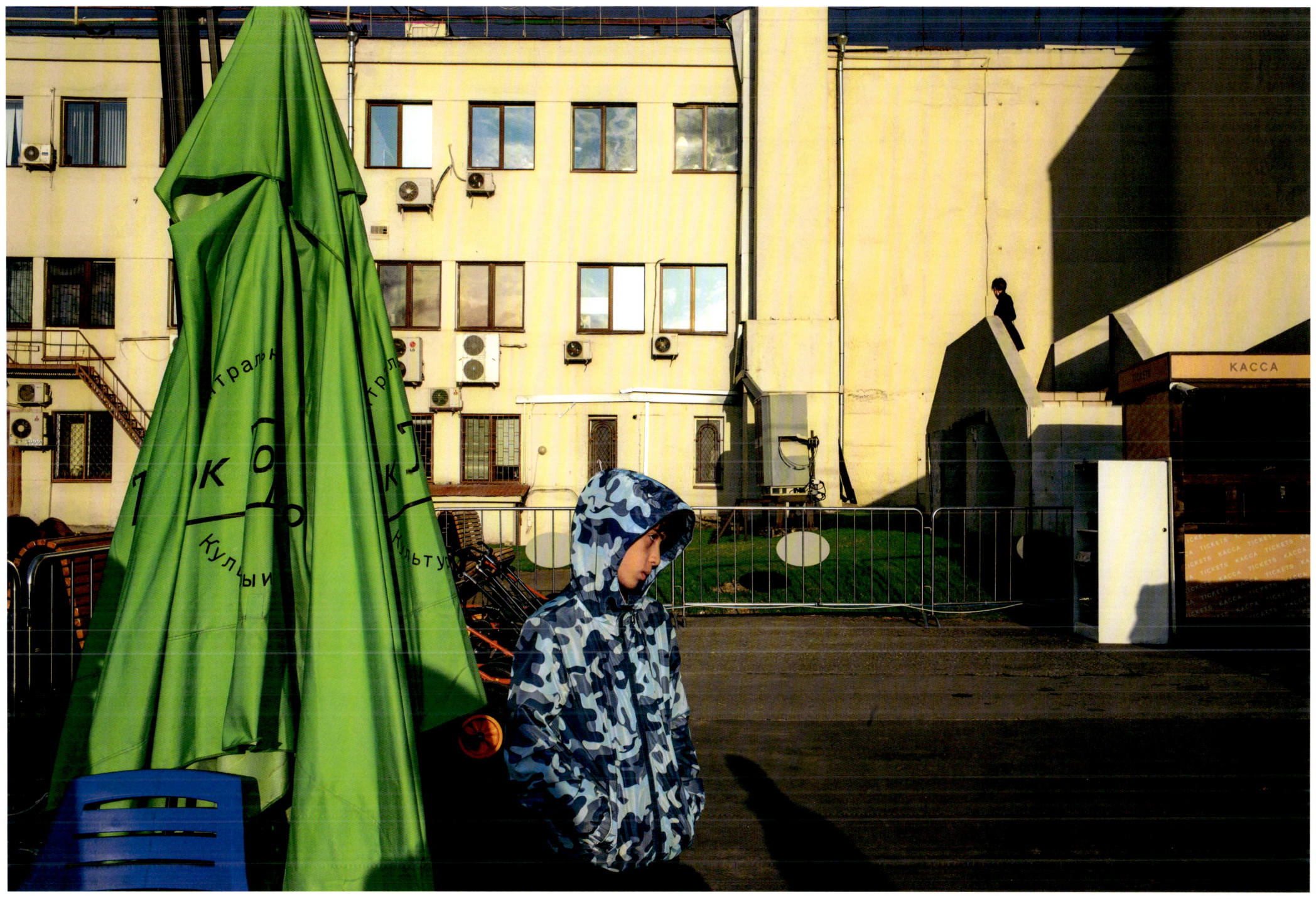

Moscow, 2019

Cincinnati, 2022

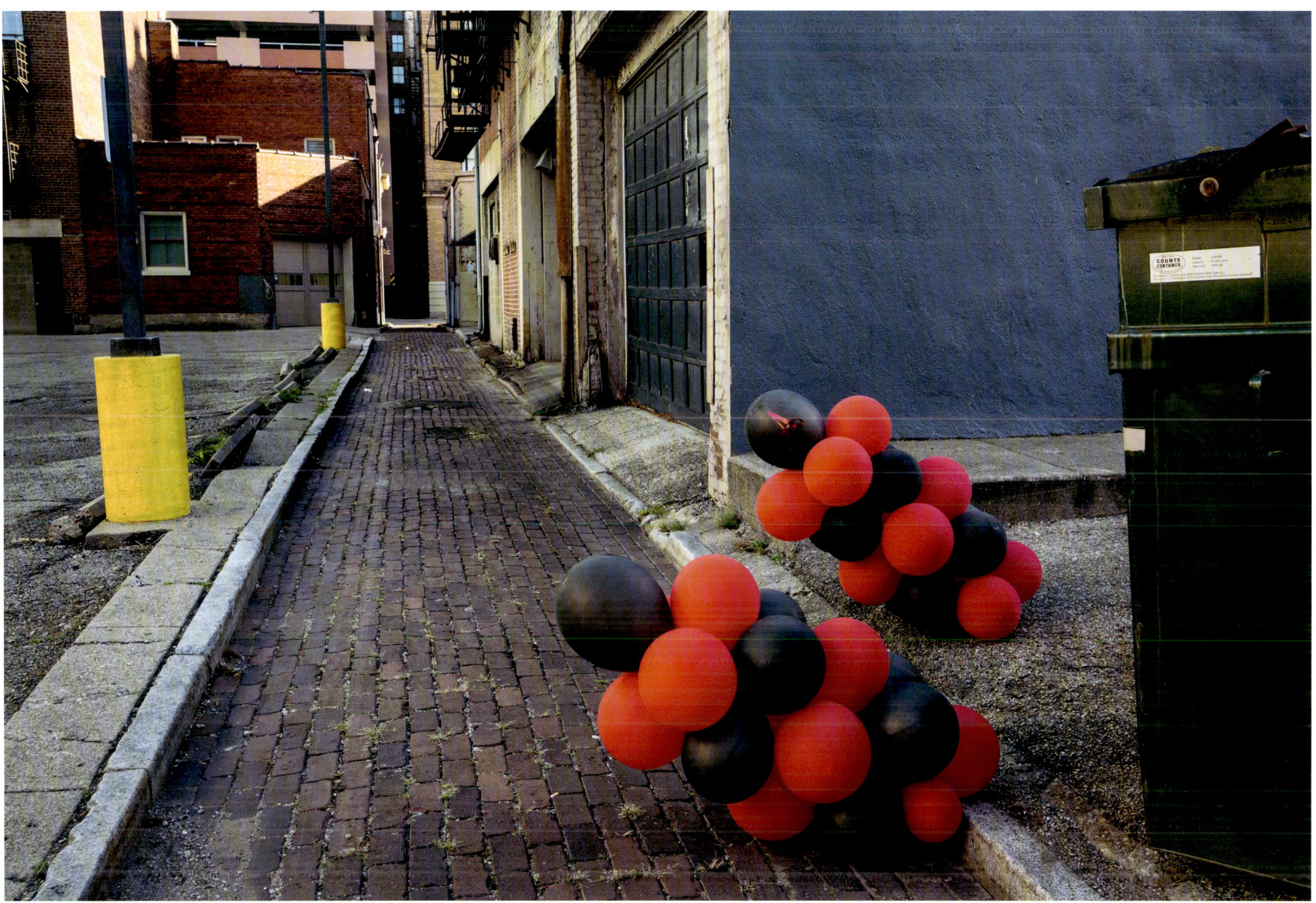

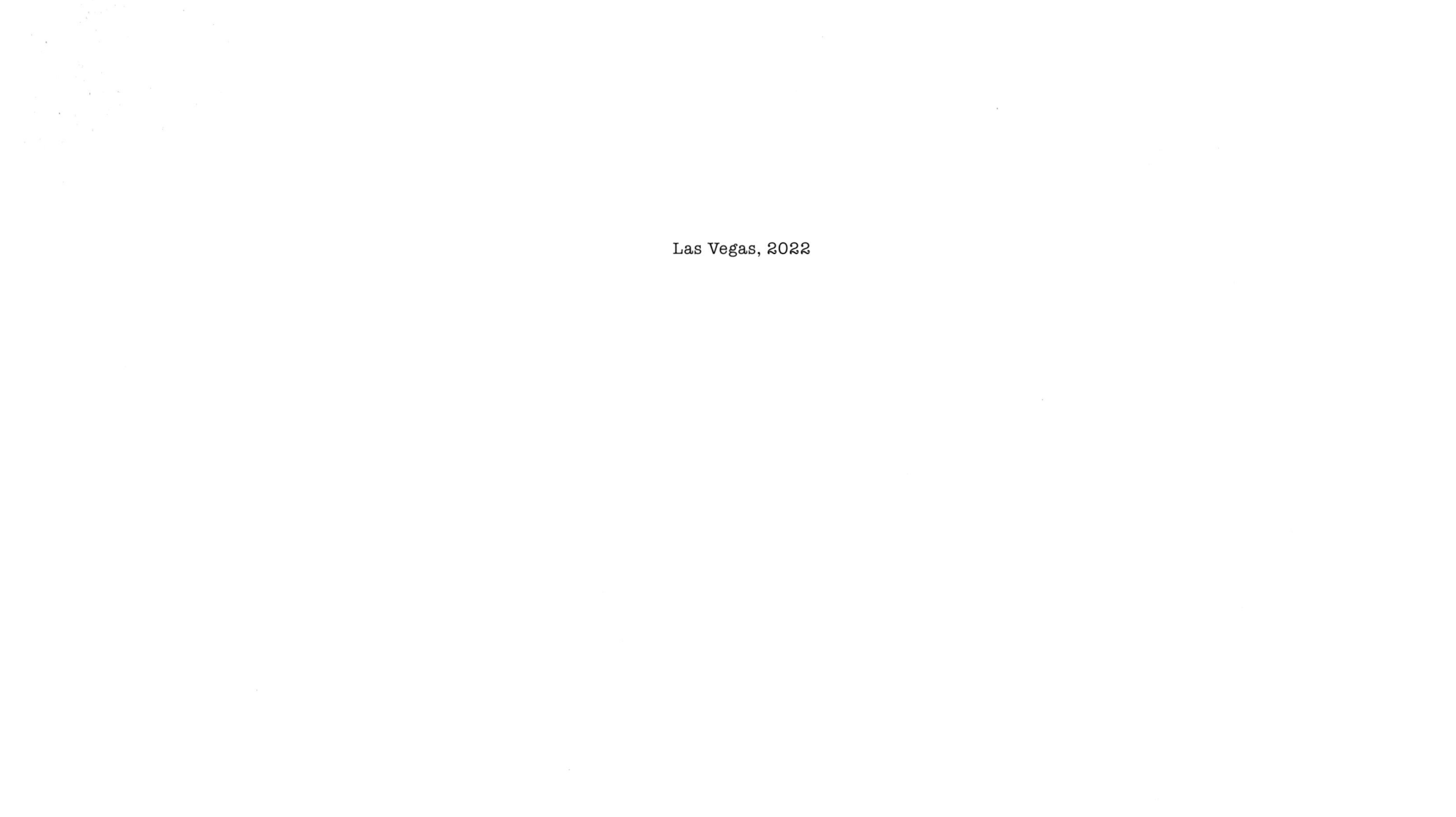

Las Vegas, 2022

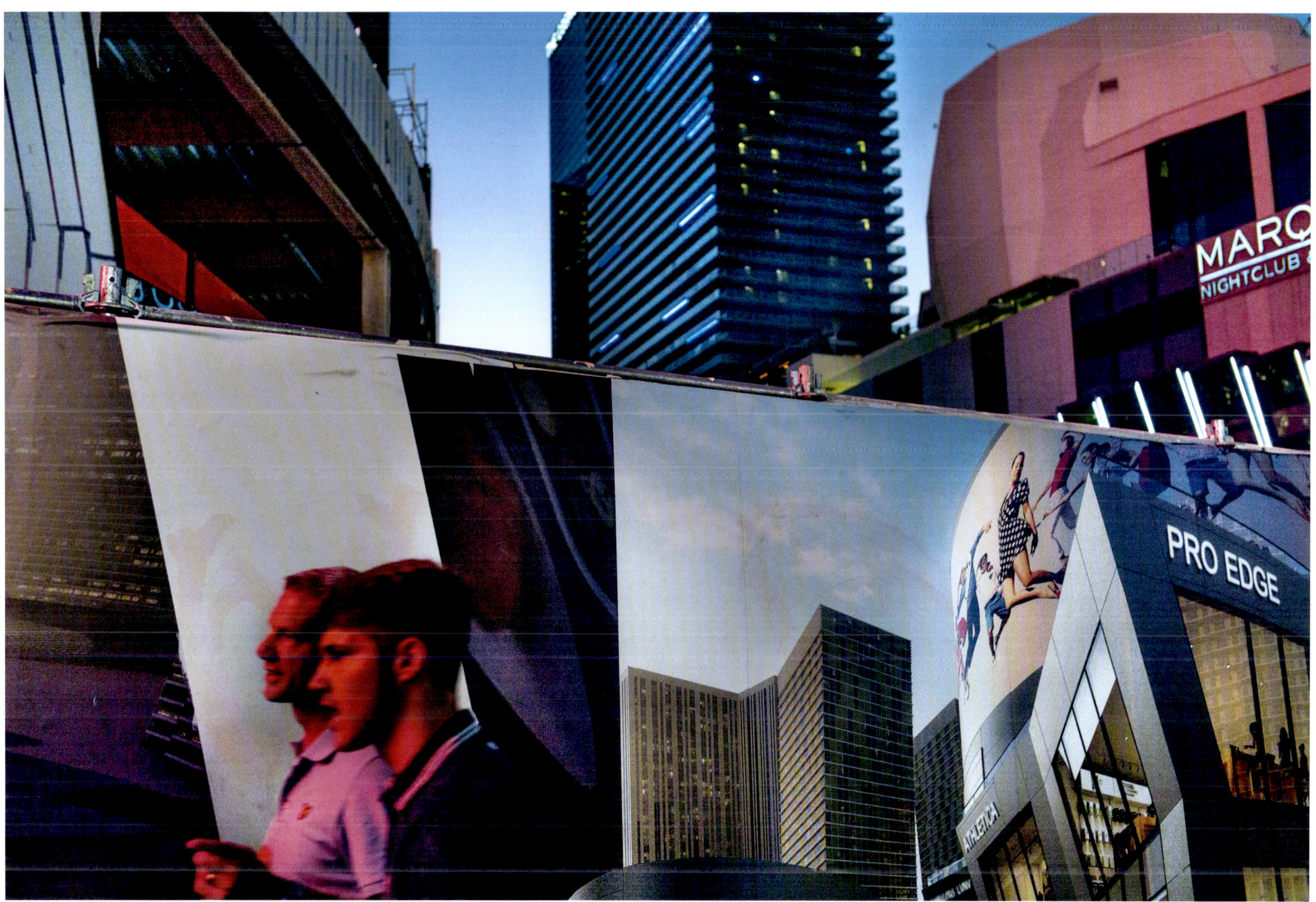

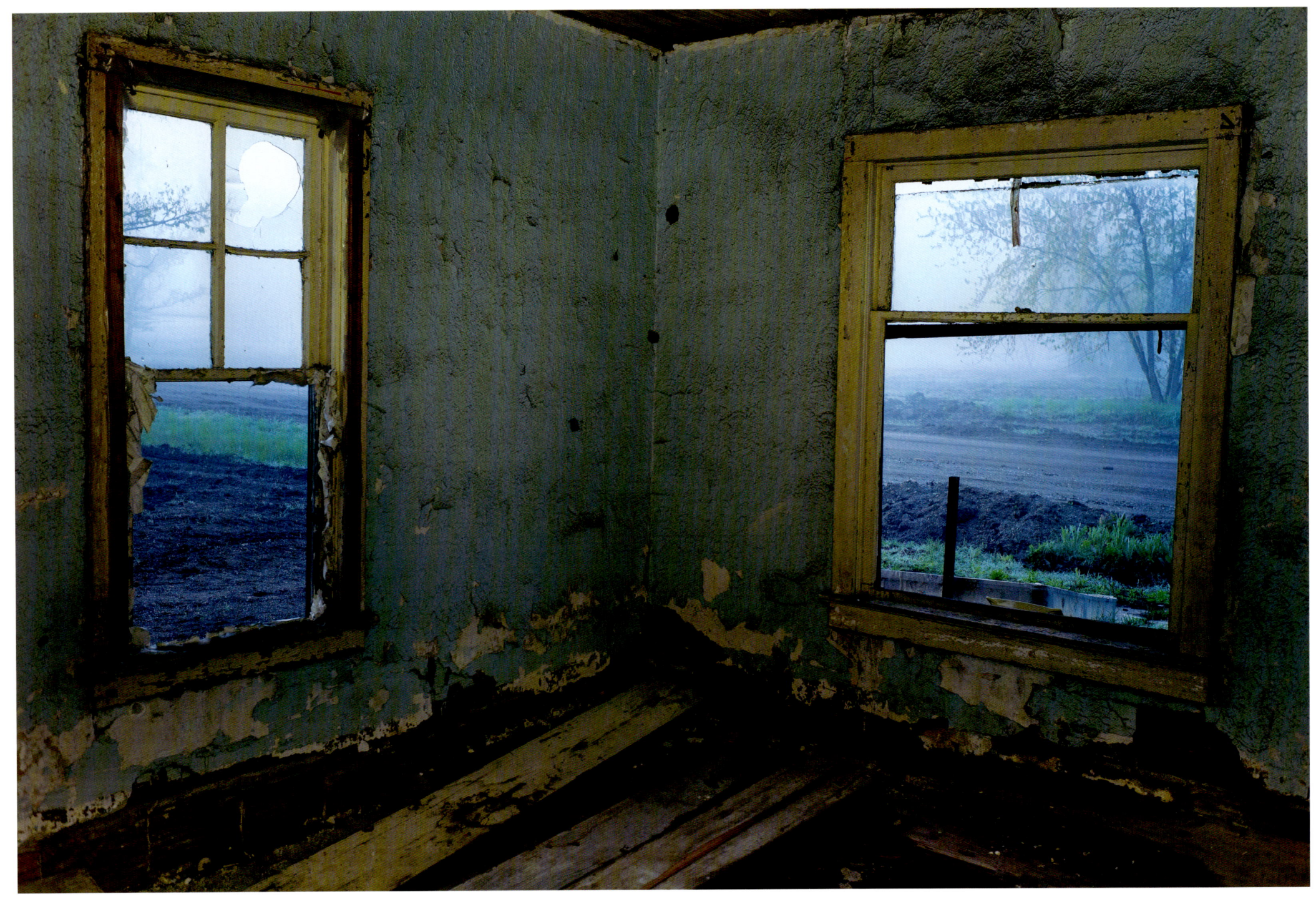

Treece, Kansas, 2012

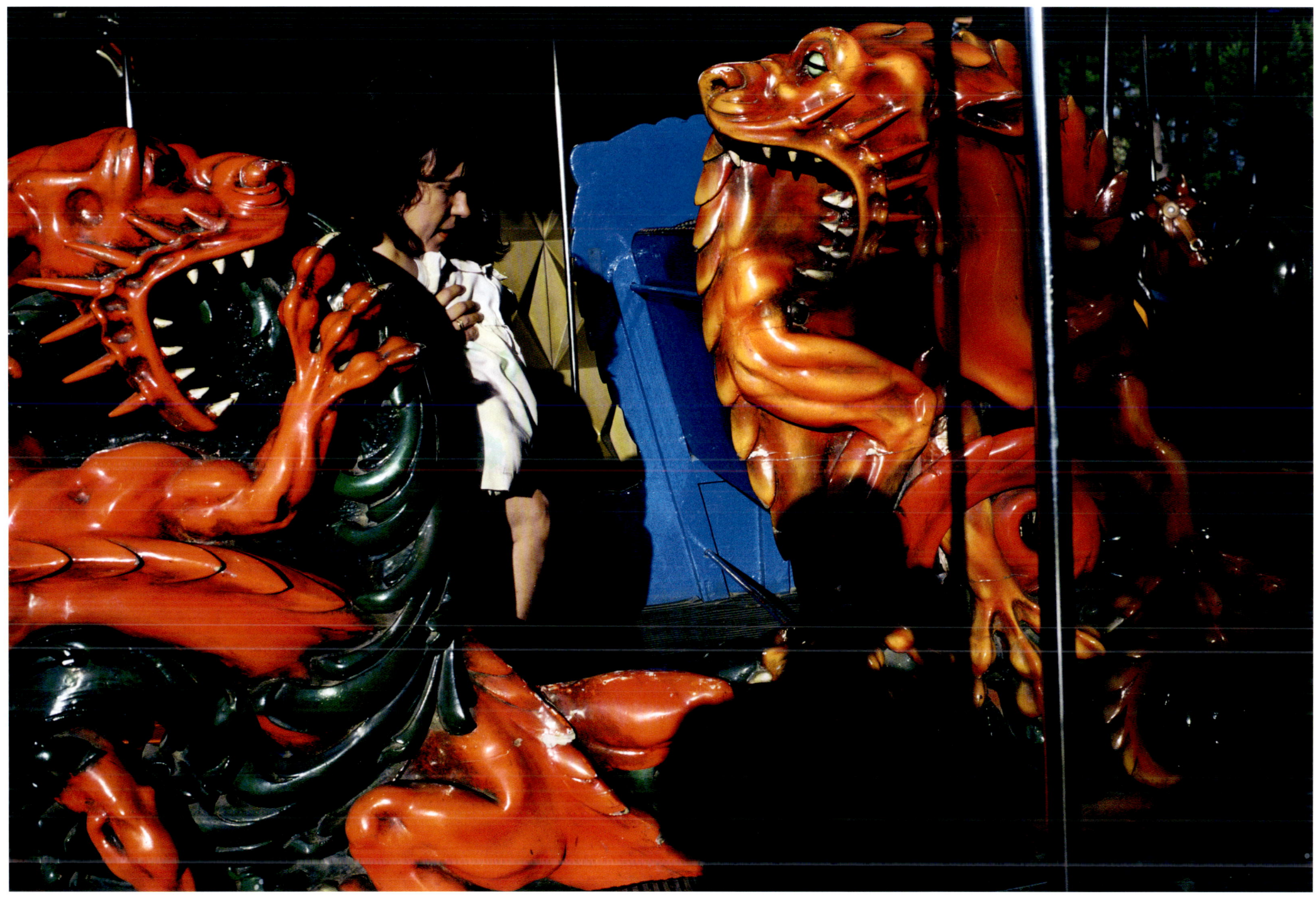

Barcelona, 1992

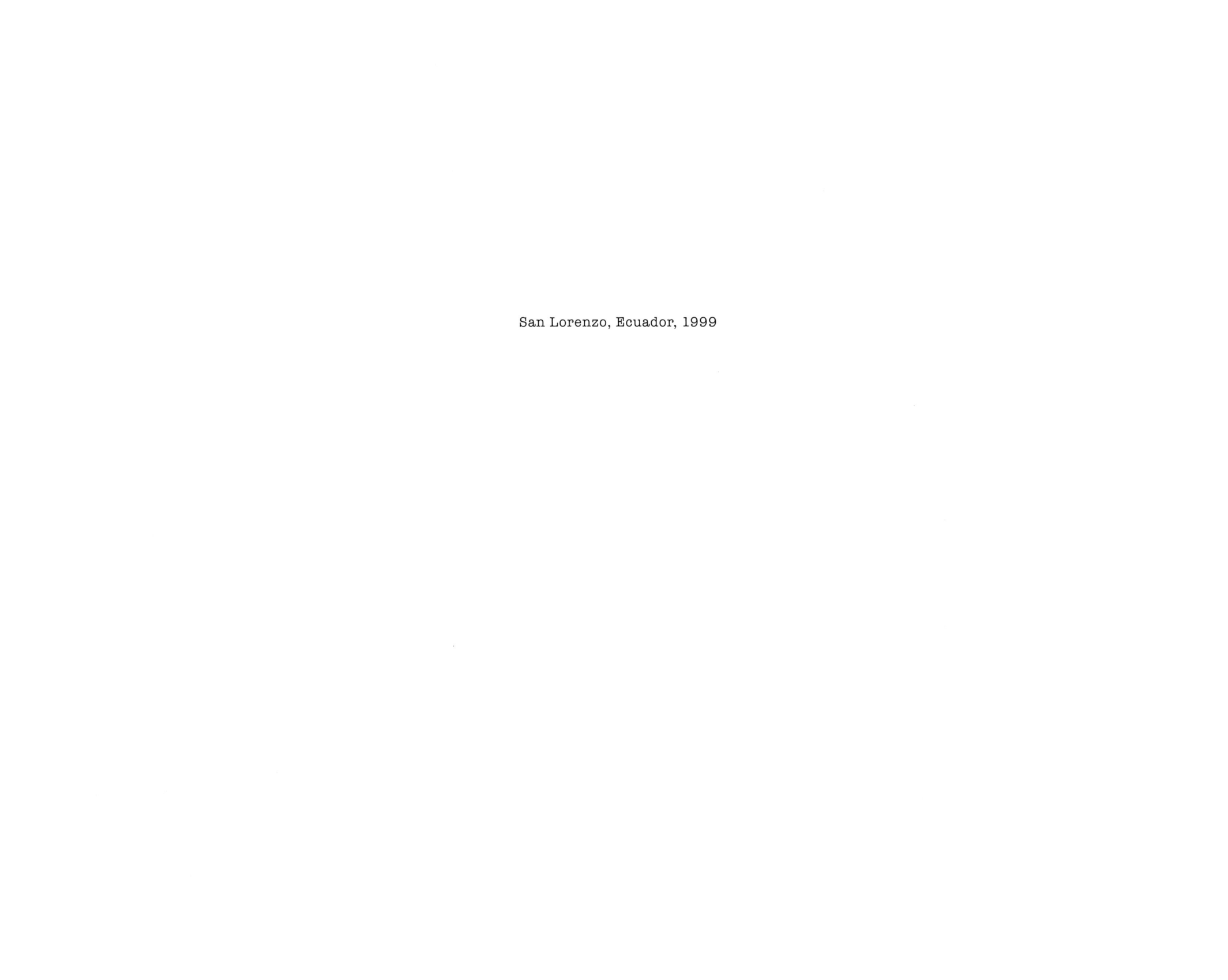

San Lorenzo, Ecuador, 1999

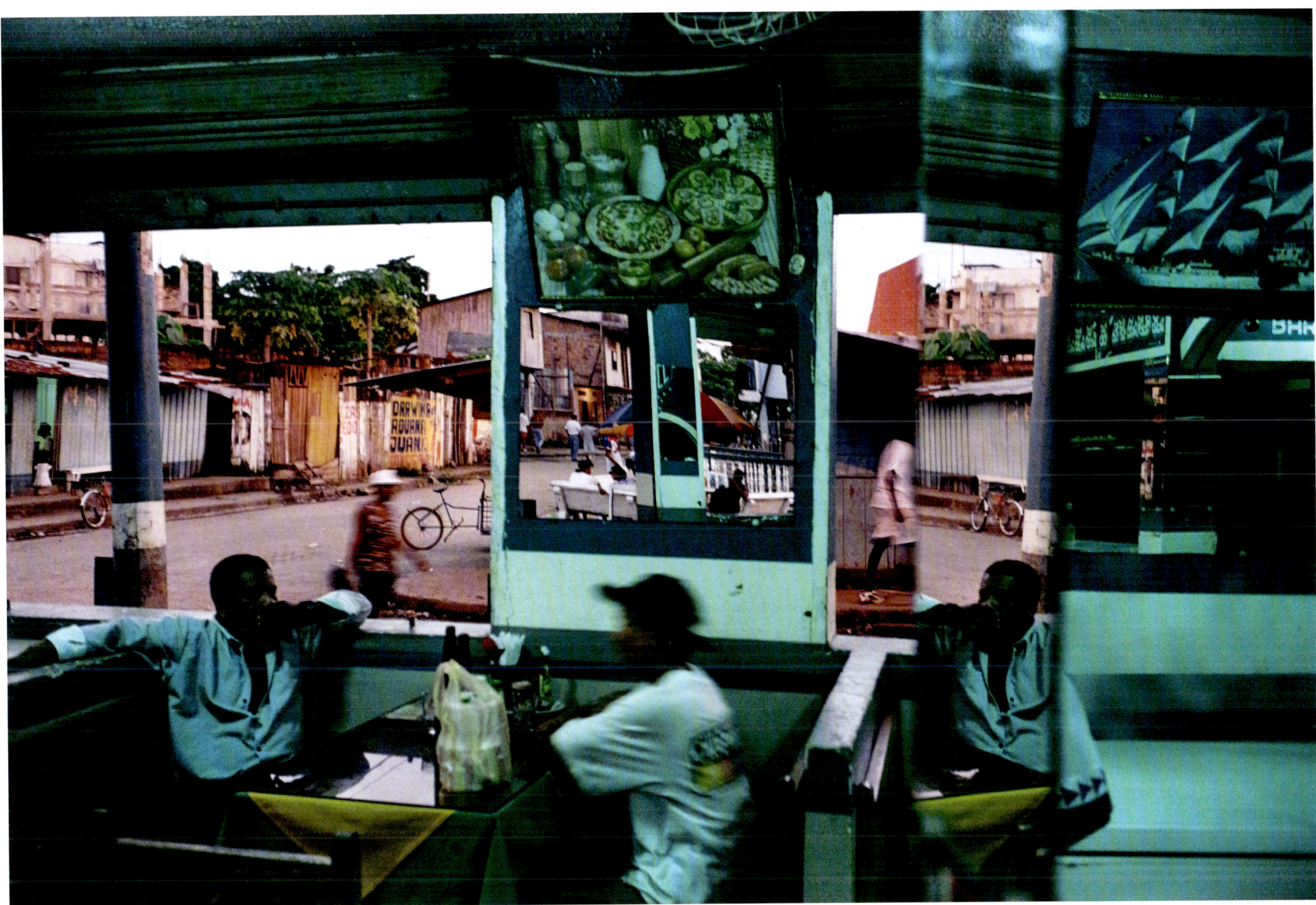

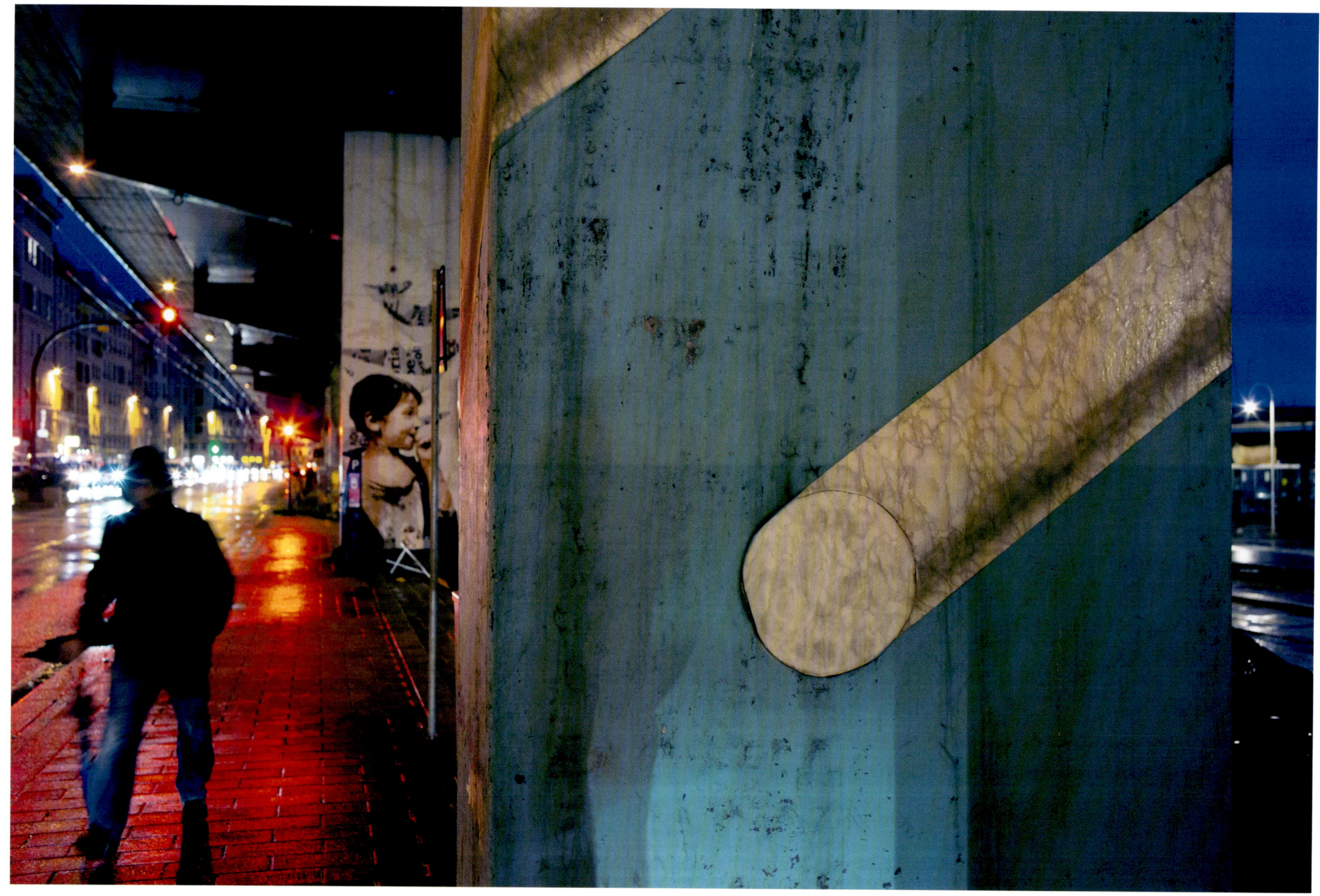

Genoa, Italy, 2019

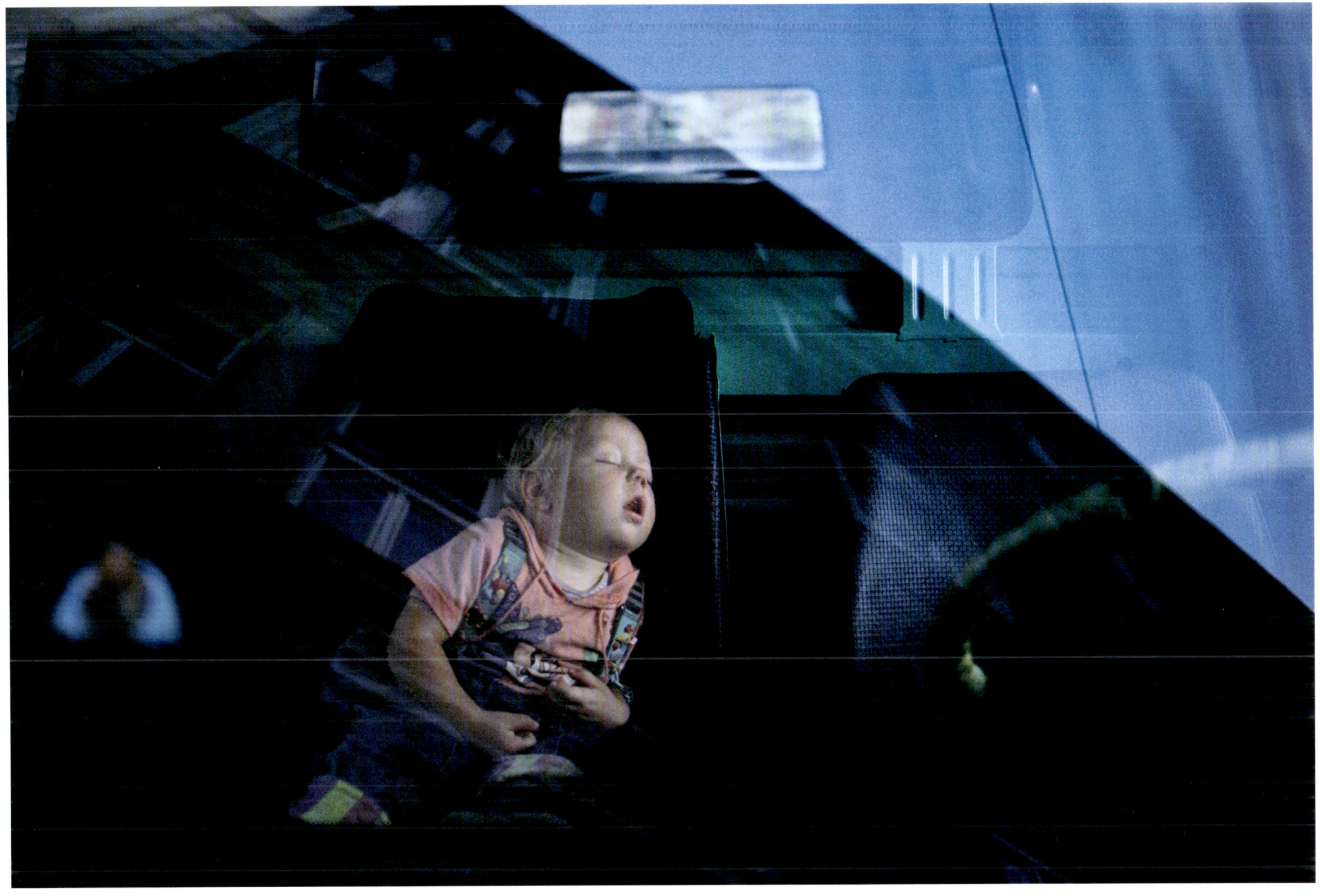

Munich, 1991

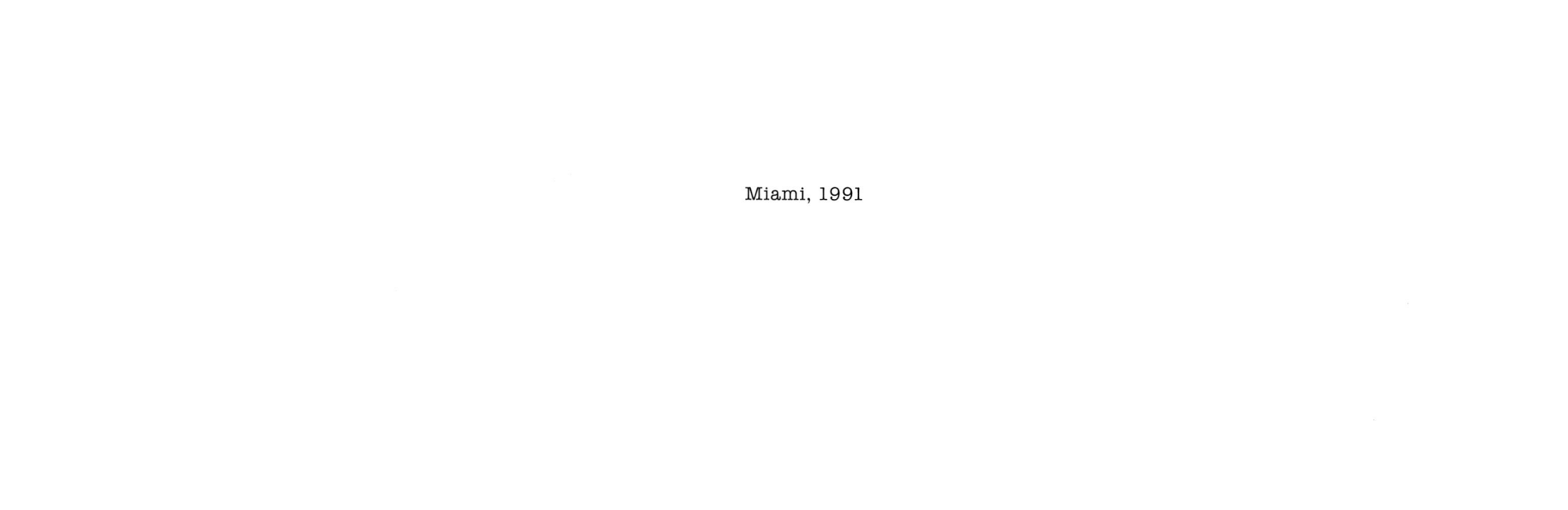

Miami, 1991

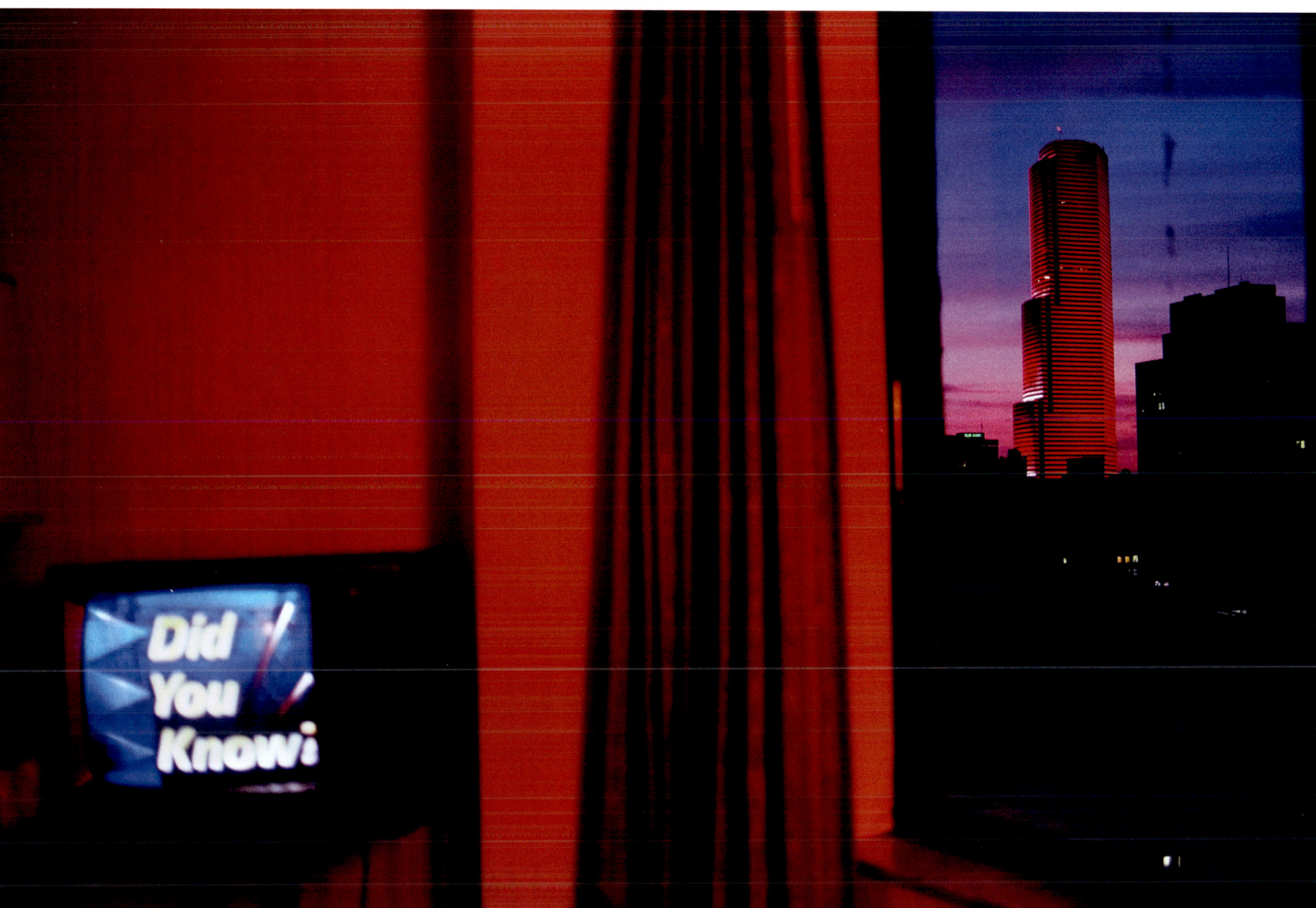

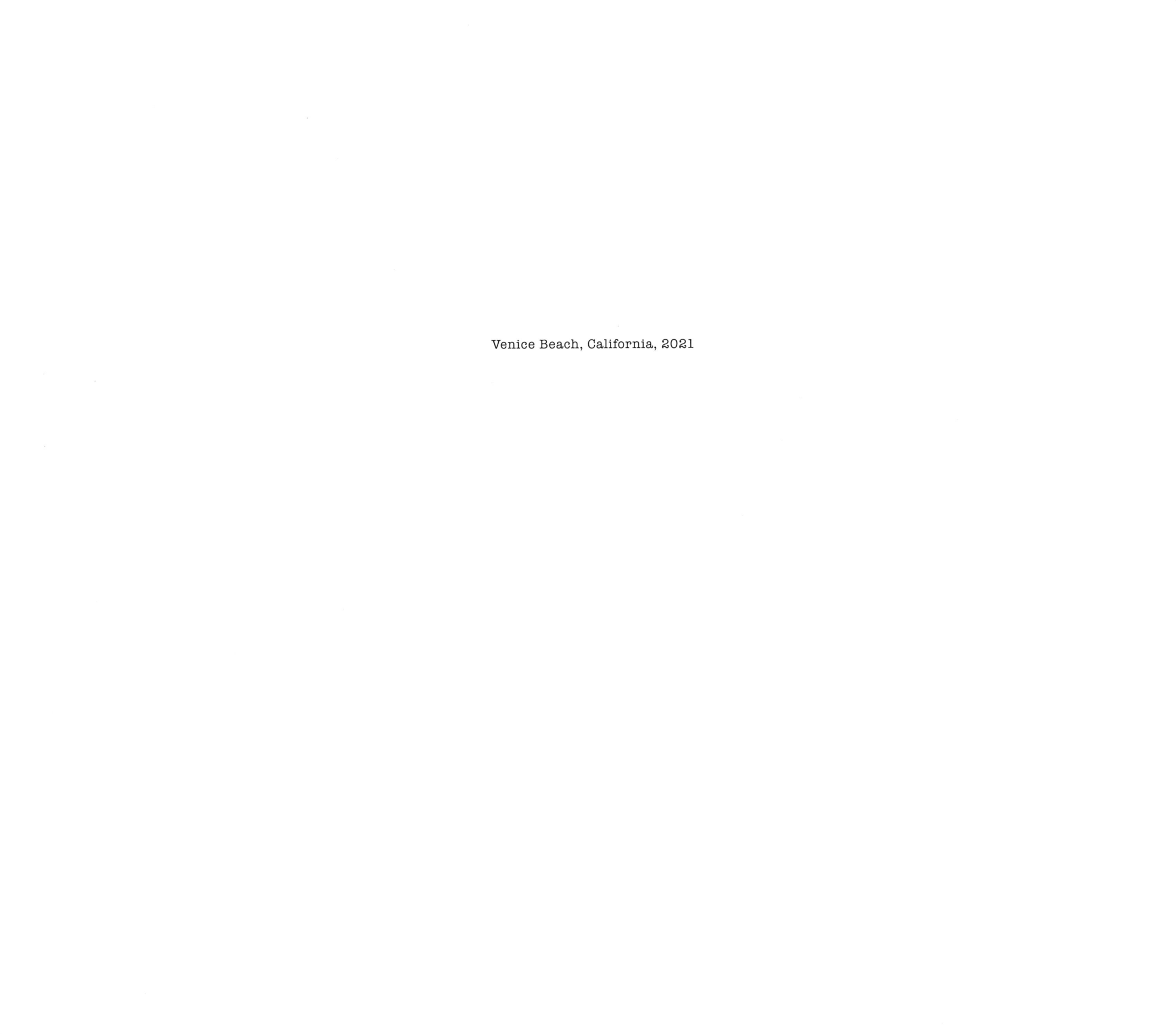

Venice Beach, California, 2021

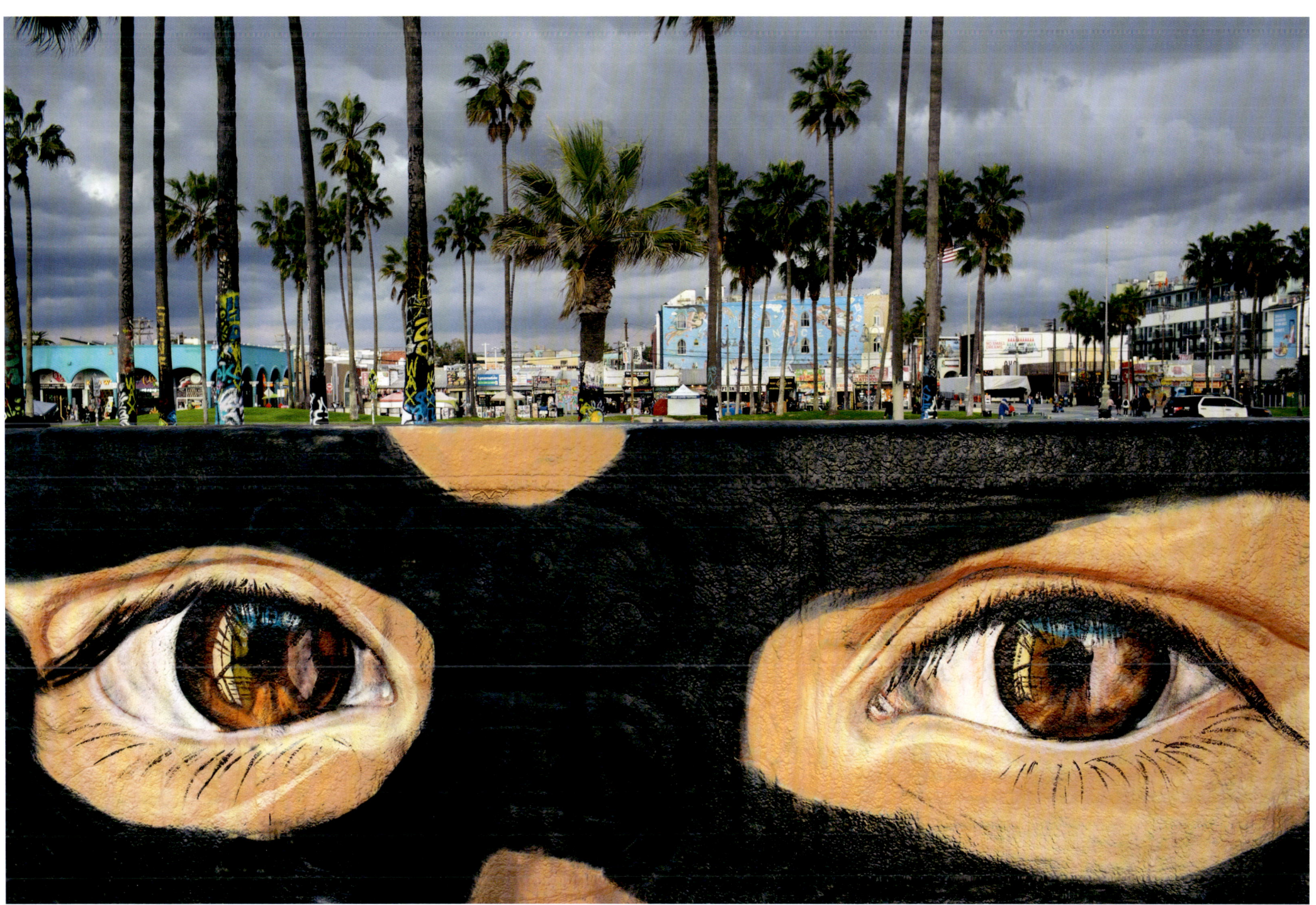

New York, 1994

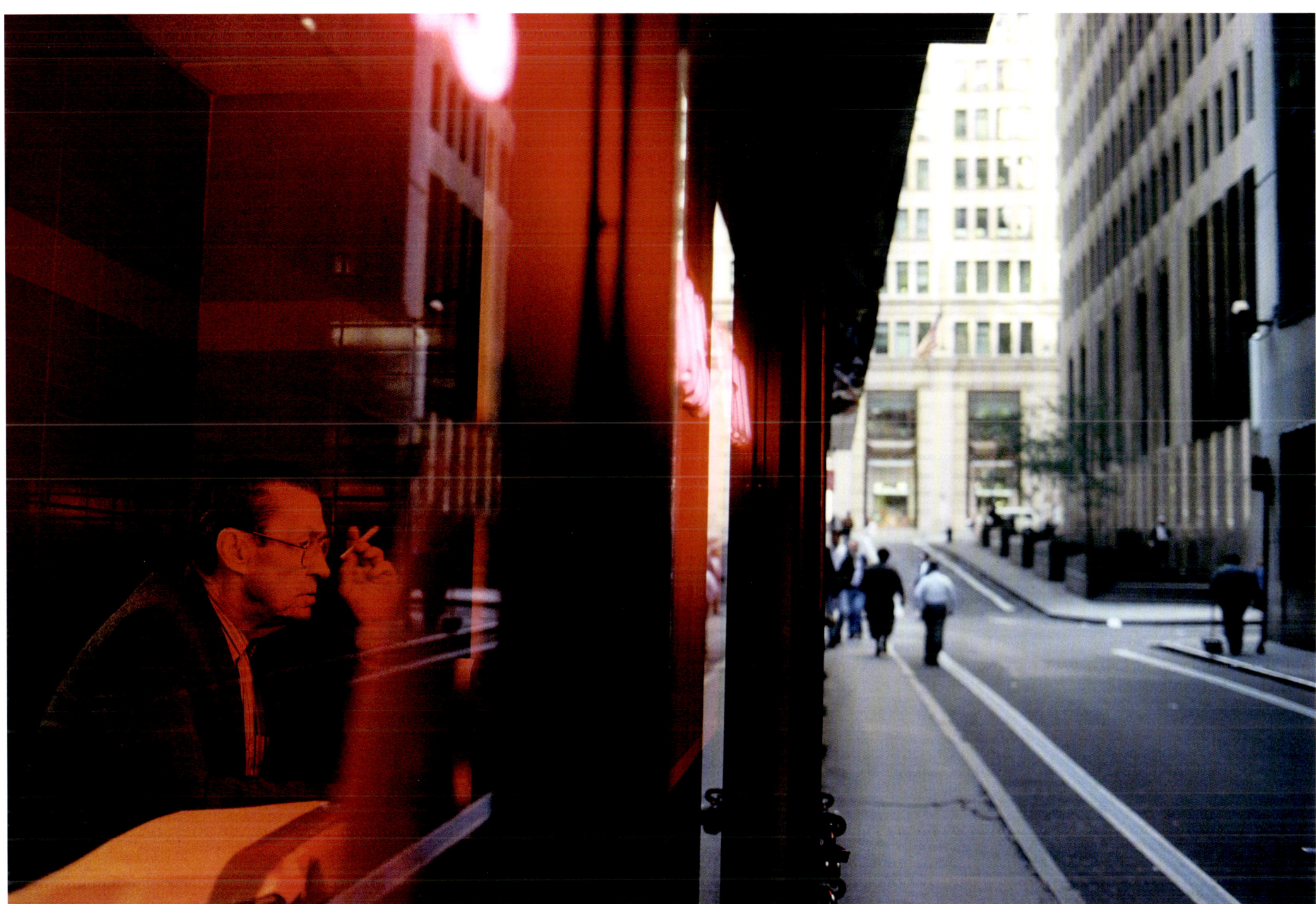

Barcelona, 1992

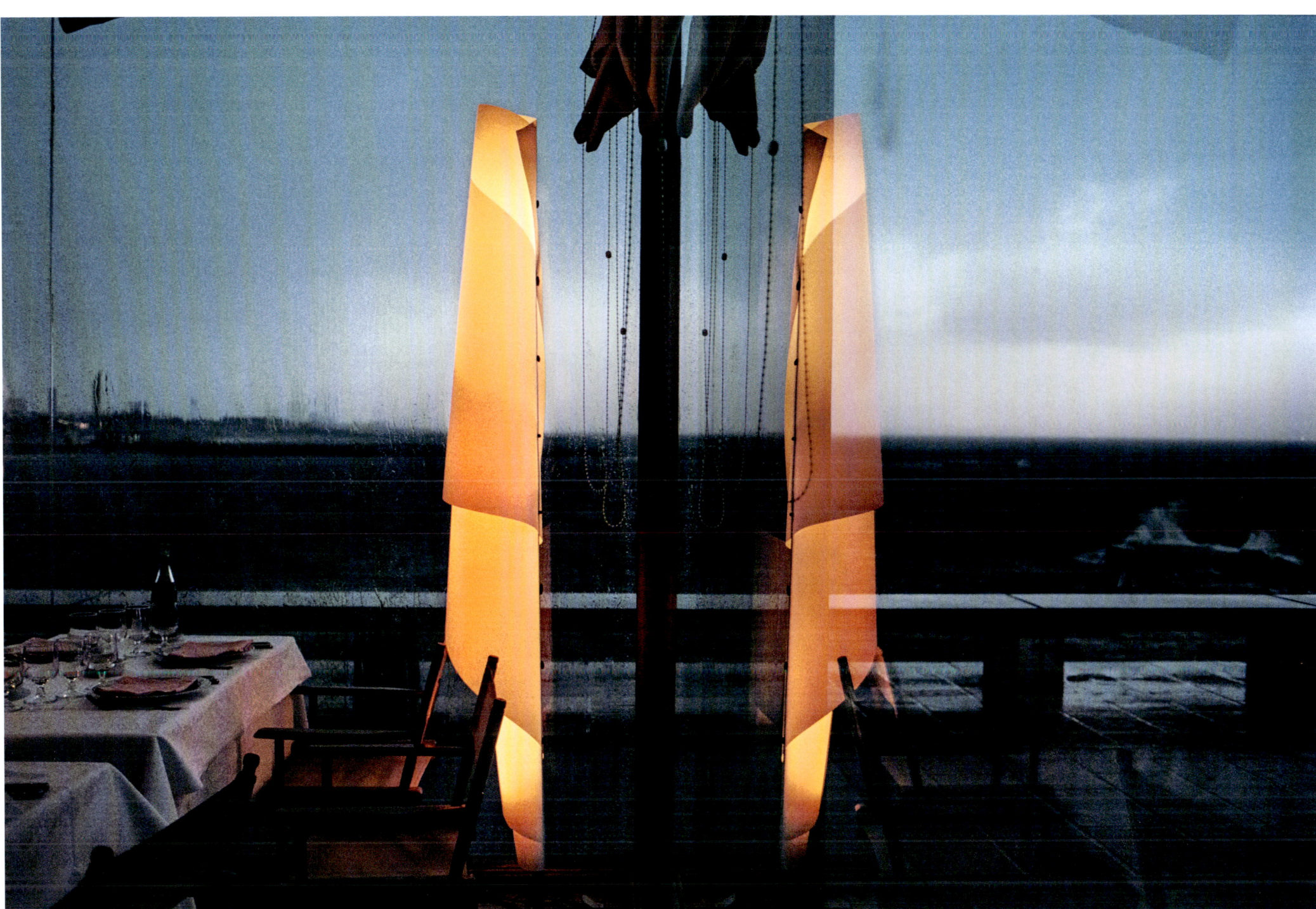

About twenty-five years ago, I was looking at a group of photographs that intrigued and somewhat puzzled me. None of these rather curious stray images had yet found their way into any of my books. It wasn't just that the photographs didn't fit the geographic parameters of the recent books I had published on Florida and the Amazon River, but also that they seemed almost placeless. As I selected and sequenced the images—seeing visual links, trying to understand the nature of the work—I began to realize that many of them struck a note of dislocation: inevitably geographically, as they were taken all over the world, but also sometimes emotionally, visually, psychologically, culturally. There was often something just a little odd, a little strange. As I shaped and expanded the sequence, it became clear that they belonged together as a single body of work.

In 1998, I was invited to publish a limited edition artist book of this work by Harvard's Film Study Center. *Dislocations* was an experiment in alternative bookmaking—a notion that seems a bit quaint these days, what with the vast variety of photographic books now being produced. *Dislocations* was printed in an edition of forty with four artist proofs. It was an accordion book with Canon laser prints (then considered state of the art) of some fifty photographs tipped in on debossed pages, with titles that I handwrote. And, it came in a unique collapsible box.

Since creating the first version, I've continued to produce other dislocated images. Three years ago, during another kind of dislocation—in sequestration for the coronavirus in the spring of 2020 in Wellfleet, Massachusetts—I started putting together this new, expanded edition on the magnetic walls of my Cape Cod studio. I began selecting images from the more than twenty years since the original publication, as well as work from the first edition and a few earlier unpublished images. This new version of *Dislocations*—with some eighty photographs made on five continents—incorporates nearly half of the original photographs from the first edition, with the lion's share comprised of later images.

Looking back, perhaps I was drawn to reimagining and enlarging this series during the pandemic in part because it was impossible to create such images in a world dominated by closed borders and disrupted travel.

—ALEX WEBB, JUNE 2023

ACKNOWLEDGMENTS

For this new edition of *Dislocations*, I'd like to thank Esteban Mauchi of Laumont Photographics for his luminous prints, David Chickey for his impeccable design, Denise Wolff of Aperture for her editorial insights—as well as the rest of the Aperture team, including Andrea Chlad for her keen production skills, Susan Ciccotti for overseeing the text, and Iola Ng for proofreading the layout. I also want to thank Tom Bollier for his fine eye and persistence in making the proofs and overseeing press production.

Lastly—and most importantly—I want to thank Rebecca Norris Webb, for her poetic sensibility in helping to select and sequence the images in this book.

I want to dedicate this book to the memory of my friends Dick Rogers (1944–2001) and Bob Gardner (1925–2014), who oversaw the creation of the first version of *Dislocations*.

—ALEX WEBB

Dislocations

Photographs and text by Alex Webb

Front cover: *Barcelona*, 1992
Back cover: *Dallas*, 1981

Editor: Denise Wolff
Designer: David Chickey
Production Director: Minjee Cho
Production Manager: Andrea Chlad
Color Separations: Thomas Bollier
Assistant Editor: Lanah Swindle
Senior Text Editor: Susan Ciccotti
Copy Editor/Proofreader: Isla Ng
Work Scholars: Isabella Convertino, Iesha E. Coppin-Forde

Additional staff of the Aperture book program includes:
Sarah Meister, Executive Director; Michael Famighetti,
Editor in Chief; Sang Patten, Managing Editor, Books;
Caroline Foulke, Editorial Assistant; Freddy Martinez,
Copy Editor/Proofreader; Karina Eckmeier, Senior Designer;
Kellie McLaughlin, Director of Sales and Outreach; Richard
Gregg, Director of Book Sales and Operations

The first edition of *Dislocations* was originally published
in 1998 by the Harvard Film Study Center in a limited
edition of forty copies.

First Aperture edition, 2023
Printed in China
10 9 8 7 6 5 4 3 2

Library of Congress Control Number:
2023907287

ISBN 978-1-59711-544-5

To order Aperture books, or inquire about
gift or group orders, contact:
orders@aperture.org

For information about Aperture trade
distribution worldwide, visit:
aperture.org/distribution

aperture

380 Columbus Avenue
New York, NY 10024
aperture.org

Aperture is a nonprofit publisher dedicated to creating
insight, community, and understanding through
photography.